This book is dedicated to the memory of my son, Sergeant Matthew Stephen Telford, Grenadier Guards, who gave his life for Queen and Country on 3rd November 2009 in Afghanistan.

He lives on in the hearts of those he loved.

MIDDLE WATERS
A Trawlerman's Tale

By
Ron Telford

Acknowledgements

I would like to express my sincere thanks to all those who have inspired and encouraged me, whilst writing this book, by following my 'blog'. I would not have had the confidence to proceed without your continued motivation. Thank you.

Special recognition goes to the following.

TOM SMITH

JOHN SMITH

BILL BUCKLEY

PETE WOODS

PETE NEVES

FRANK POOK

DAVID ORNSBY [of the Grimsby Heritage Centre]

STEVE FARROW

PETER GREENE

DENNIS AVERY

FRED POWLES

DAVID POWLES

JANE HYLDON KING

MATTY McCOURT

CHERYL TELFORD [Wife]

I also have to mention the enthusiasm and encouragement I have received from numerous people who have read my 'blog'.

Thank you for your support.

Contents

Introduction

The stories and memories I am writing about happened over fifty years ago. I don't always remember what I did yesterday but these memories come flooding back whilst I am working as a tour guide on the Ross Tiger.

Having come from a fishing family myself, I often feel that the sea is in my blood.

I may not get things, such as the date or time of year completely right, however, I'm never, ever wrong about what actually happened. I recall incidents that are as clear as the day they happened.

The traditions and practices of this period should be documented so that future generations are aware of the type of men who experienced hardship and discomfort in order to earn a living and put fish on our table.

The men who sailed at this time are ageing and there will be no one left to remember how 'it used to be'. There will be a day when my story is finished (but not just yet).

We must never forget our proud HERITAGE as Grimsby was once the BIGGEST FISHING PORT IN THE WORLD with over 400 trawlers and 7,000 people employed in the dock area!!

A Poem written by Matty McCourt

A FISHERMAN'S LIFE

I COME FROM A GREAT TOWN
A TOWN NAMED GREAT GRIMSBY
"When boats were made of Wood
The men were made of STEEL
Boys became young men before their time
The WOMEN, the LOVE of a thousand Aphrodites
When HOMES were made from LOVE
AND GREAT GRIMSBY ONE BIG FAMILY"

Here is my story!

1

Boston Kestrel

Having been to sea on the Boston Concord, freezing our balls off for 27 days, dock to dock, landing in Hull, coming home on the ferry and running aground on a sand bank, it had not been a good time all-round.

Poor Alf had been left near the ferry and I had put him on a barrow to take him to the train platform and watched, open mouthed, as the train pull away leaving us stranded. I had telephoned the wife, who drove a good hour or so to pick us up. When she picked us up, she had our son in the back of the car. Alf sat alongside him, unable to put a sentence together. He frightened my son to death. We arrived in Grimsby and managed to drop Alf off at his house. He opened the garden gate and entered his home.

Things did not improve, as the next day, I arrived down dock to discover that we had landed in debt. The cashier seemed to wrangle my tax, giving me rebate. I finally saw the ships runner who told me to take all my gear off the ship, as she would not be sailing again.

With not even a fry of fish to take home I ventured to the Clee Park (pub). Having had two or three pints I eventually went home, asking myself; 'What will I do now? A couple of days later I received a telephone call asking me if I would like to sail in the Boston Kestrel fishing at the Westwards. Hooray! Good News at last but this didn't last long.

After taking my gear off the Boston Concord I put it directly on to the Boston Kestrel which was berthed on the North Wall. This was completely full of ships tied up nose to nose as ICELAND had increased their fishing limits to 200 miles. All the top earners had been laid up apart from just a handful which were still working at the Norwegian Coast.

It had been a sad day whilst taking my gear off the Boston Concord and putting it on to the KESTREL but at least I am in work. Many, at this time, are in limbo and at an age where they may not get any other employment. Rumours are going around that most of the deep-sea trawlers are going to be sold or scrapped. I wondered who will be buying them!

Sailing orders were received for Wednesday a.m. We are having to do a couple of days work on her changing her from deep-water trawling to mid-water and we would be going to sea with a crew of ten men.

Skipper Derek Brown

Mate Jim Donnelly

Third Hand [Me] Ron Telford

Deckie Linnet Legs, Johnny Walker, Jimmy Walker, Bryner Newland

Cook, Pete Bowman

Chief Engineer Nev Snowdon/Plus Second Engineer /Greaser Cleggy Kinnaird

Seems strange as I sailed in this ship on its maiden voyage from Grimsby. I was in her later when our son was born in October 1972. I am in her now going on shares.

Ordered for sailing at 0300 hours but finally picked up at 0345 hours. I spent nearly an hour pacing up and down in the lounge. Several cars passed by with me thinking it was for me and then thinking the taxi wasn't coming at all. When it did finally arrive, I put my gear into the car and then went back inside to say my goodbyes to my loved ones.

When we reached the dock, I put my gear on board and then popped into the outfitters for stores, gloves, reading, gutting knife, with other odds and ends. The time came to sail and I was called to the bridge. With a few mutterings we sailed. All lined up for the lock gates when, out of the accommodation, one of the deckies threw his gear on the quay and then jumped off himself. Luckily, he didn't fall in the dock or injure himself.

We headed for the anchorage and waited for a couple of hours when the Alfred Bannister (which was a tug) called us up on the radio saying that he had a new crew member for us. I went on the deck to receive the new deckie and it was Cleggy Kinnaird who sailed as either cook, engineer or deckie. I soon discovered that he was pissed. I told a crew member to get him inside and to get him to roll in. What a great start to the trip! I took the first watch until breakfast and had a couple of rounds of toast as no one had been in the galley. I turned in and after a couple of hours all hell broke loose!!!

I was awoken suddenly to lots of shouting, I quickly discovered that one of the crew members had become aggressive after having a few cans and drams and was now running around with a fire axe. He had gotten into the steering flat but he was so drunk that he couldn't do much damage. Another crew member and I managed to take the axe off him and stayed with him. The Skipper contacted Whitby Harbour who sent a couple of Police out on their pilot boat and he was handed over with the help of our crew. This trip seemed doomed somehow and we were later informed that a replacement would be sent to Aberdeen to join us.

The Skipper came down searching for any booze and what he discovered he emptied overboard. After the events the 'Brave Faces' appeared saying that we should have called for help with the situation. This happened right **next to their Cabins!** I imagine that they were messing themselves!

I laid down again until teatime which soon came around. We had lamb chops, mashed potato and peas with gravy which went down a treat. I grabbed a couple of hours before going on watch at 2300 hours. I am already feeling tired before we've even started the hard graft! Just after tea time we picked up the new crew member via Aberdeen Pilot cutter. Let's hope things soon get back to NORMALITY.

On watch and heading towards Duncansby Head. We should be there early morning and hopefully fishing before lunchtime. I came off watch at 2300 hours without any incident. The weather had been fresh steaming North with the Daymen not able to get on the deck. Breakfast time and all hands called out for something to eat and drink and we then ventured onto the deck. We are just passing Fair Isle, destination just off Fouler, where reports are saying average fish being caught is about 50 baskets mixed cod, coley and haddock.

We have just put the otter boards over the side and hung over on their chains. I've just tied the Cod line and with a bit of time left we released the ships washer and put up the holding frame. The skipper shouted out that we can put the gear over the side. All the lashing/chains had been taken off in preparation. First the cod ends went over, with the rest of the net soon following. Next the bobbins went and soon enough, we began lowering the doors away. Soon we were paying the warps away, both warps were now in the towing block and finally we were all square.

Time for a quick smoke and cuppa then back on the deck to finish putting the washer up. We untied the lashings using a couple of lifting straps and we commenced to lift the washer into place. We started to take the weight on the straps when suddenly the washer slid on the deck and landed on my ankle. I screamed out in pain and the washer was then lifted off my foot. The pain was excruciating and I started to feel dizzy. I was carried off the deck and taken into the messdeck. The Skipper came to see me and gave me a couple of painkillers which didn't help at all. The cook came and gave me a sweet tea.

Soon the trawl was being heaved up and we were soon making our way into Lerwick. I'm now sitting in the messdeck, going over, in my head what had happened with my accident, when the 2nd engineer came up out of the engine room with an injured hand. The Skipper was informed and was not very happy. Just before teatime we were taken to Lerwick Hospital where they looked at both of us. They don't think that I have broken anything but I had badly bruised my ankle. The engineer had broken his wrist though and so we were both taken to the seaman's mission. I was taken to a room where my personal gear had been placed ready for me, including my bond. I had something light to eat and had been given plenty of painkillers.

I began to settle down when the Skipper came to give me some travel arrangements. We were being picked up tomorrow morning and flying home via Fred Parkes own private plane which was a Piper Cherokee. I seem to remember the registration was **B D S F 1**. The next morning, we were picked up to join the plane and two new crew members had been sent up for our replacement.

WE HAD BEEN AT SEA FOR FIVE DAYS!

WE HAD NOT CAUGHT A SINGLE FISH DURING THIS TIME!

WE HAD FOUR CREW CHANGES!

Now beginning to wonder whether I will be going back to sea. Well at least I have a few smokes with my Bond. Just over a week later I sailed on the Boston Halifax. As the saying goes, 'You can't keep a good man down!'

Random Memory

Remembering as a child playing marbles in our street. When a fisherman walked down towards us, he would scatter the oddments of change from his pockets. We always called him 'uncle' and he usually gave my dad a fry of fish.

A fisherman I recall who scattered cash was Fred Philipson who sailed as mate, as well as skipper. There was another fisherman I remember because he was called William Shakespeare and he sailed as chief engineer. When he saw us, he always told us to 'Fuch orf'. I wonder if that's why I didn't have many friends who were engineers. I have only a handful that I continue to call friends.

Random Memory

When we started courting a certain crew member who was a deckhand asked Cheryl Telford; 'What are you doing messing about with a deckie? You should be going out with a skipper or mates' son.' Although annoyed by the remark we just ignored him because I said he'd had too much to drink and it was a wind up. When we sailed, I let him know that I was not happy with his remark and gave him a piece of my mind, with maybe something else as well but I'm not saying here.

Random Memory

I can remember a certain landing day when the crew met up in the White Knight having a few drinks and a good time. We each took it in turns to buy a round. A certain woman who had been in our company asked, as each person bought a round, for a bag of crisps with her drink and everyone obliged. This went on for about 6 rounds and when it was my turn to go to the bar, she asked the same question; 'Can I have a bag of crisp as well?'. I said to the bar person; 'Just give her an effing box full.' much to the amusement of everyone there but she didn't ask for any more.

Random Memories

REMEMBER the quarter rope gear. Told to chuck the rope off the cleats. The deckie learner was in a dream world. He was caught in tight. I'm glad that I had just sharpened a piece of hatch batten as with one swipe of the blade the rope parted, releasing the deckie learner at the rail. He did thank me and I replied that when we bring the net back in you can splice the effing quarter rope, which he did. Every time we repeated the job he would shout out; **'I'm all clear!'** Lesson learned.

Random Memories
Ross Renown Circa 1970/71

When I was a deckhand I can remember sailing in the Renown with Big Bag, Barry McCall. What a gentleman he was! He always said please and thank you. I never saw him rattled and by, what a clever fisherman. He reminded me of a great friend who recently passed away Raymond Evans.

I remember joining the vessel with (big nose) Lenny Bruce, Roy Page, Big Albert Walker, Tony Lawrence, Tom Jones (cook) with a few more names that I have forgotten at this moment in time.

I can recall getting out of the Taxi, climbing up a steep ladder, then up over the ships rail. I am now on top of the whaleback proceeding to the stern of the ship towards the after end, stepping over a large step and I then followed a ship mate who directed me to my sleeping quarters.

This ship had a great atmosphere. You could feel it in the air. I put all my gear away and went ashore to the local ship's outfitters. I personally liked Coleridge's where one of the men had the same name as me - 'Ron'. He always greeted us with a smile and yes, I know that he had been after my money but a little banter went along way with me. Not like that little arsehole in Vincent's 'Eric', the little smiling knobhead. I wonder how many times he had put extra payments in for unknowing punters, as he had tried to do with me.

I am now back on board the ship and soon big nose, the mate, told me that I would be on watch with the bosun, Barry Almond who was, another very quietly spoken man. Later on in my career I sailed with both his brothers Pete, as mate in Boston's and Freddy (Pink Panther) also in Boston's.

A short while later the mate had left when the order came to let go. A couple of us pulling up the ships ladders which were soon taken off us to be stowed away. We gently made our way towards the lock gates. I had been given a rope fender to shield the ship between ourselves and the lock gates. I seem to remember that they were not used and no sooner had I put the fender away and we pulled the yo yo arm out, put up the ship's washer in position. I was just about to walk off the deck when I was called back on to the main deck where four sets of bridles, 40 fathom, two x 50s and 70s fathom which had to be pulled through the port alleyway along the accommodation, then through an extra-large porthole (Escape Hatch). They were then stowed in a large area and hung up with labels detailing size. This place had been known as the Bingo Room.

Lunchtime soon arrived and the cook had prepared a decent meal. I seem to remember him standing outside the galley with his clean apron on. He was another fine Gentleman with whom I had a few good yarns, during the voyage.

Random Memory

I clearly remember a particular trip whilst on the Boston Phantom. On leaving Grimsby, on a dinner time sailing, the weather forecast had not been in our favour. A Northerly Gale was forecast imminently. The good old watchman had been on the ball with a pan of shackles shimmering away on top of the diesel stove.

I have done my bit so far, by taking the ship out of the dock but as we were approaching the spurn light ship the Mate relieved me. He told me to get myself battened down when I turn in. I had a good meal from the big pan of shackles, my gear was put away and I was all wedged up in my cabin WHEN I was awoken from a deep sleep by the sound of strange voices coming from near the cook's cabin. I also heard a few other noises and a few sounds of laughter. On opening my cabin door and wiping the sleep from my eyes, I ventured out of my berth. Four or five of the lads were crammed in near the cook's door. I slowly peered over one of the crew's shoulders and saw the cook who seemed to be in a world of his own. He was talking in riddles and then making out that somebody was chasing him. I had seen this behaviour a few times previously always known as Dee Tees it means 'delirium tremens' which usually occurs due to alcohol withdrawal. Our cook had been in hospital after opening his mouth to someone bigger than him in a pub. With the combination of drink and hospital treatment he had lost the plot, as it were.

I went on the bridge and informed the mate who went to investigate for himself. On his return he informed the skipper, who soon got onto the ships radio and talking to a doctor. The advice given was to get the man ashore as quickly as possible and not to leave the cook by himself. Arrangements were made to put the man ashore in Blythe and await a new cook who would travel up by taxi. As soon as we had tied up an Ambulance had been waiting for us and two persons came on board and took the cook away. To this day I can still see the crazy glare of his eyes as he was led away into the Ambulance.

How strange, where we were tied up, just around the Quay, there was a pub which I think it was called the Dun Cow or some name similar. The crew were allowed to go for a pint or two and just after midnight, effing sizer appeared with Pete Bowman a cook who I had sailed with on many occasions.

By 0200 hours we had sailed and I volunteered to take the watch until breakfast as the Mate and Skipper had been up most of the day. At least I had had a couple hours sleep but by breakfast time I could hardly keep my eyes open. The first day out of dock and I'm feeling knackered already. The weather had been freshening all morning. I left it up to the Mate if he wanted to call the daymen out.

2

Boston Halifax

I was called back to the runner's office and was asked to go in the Boston Halifax which was sailing to the westward in a few days' time. Oh, what a relief! With all the ships being laid up at least I had another ship to sail in. I am feeling elated as I thought Raymond Evans would be taking us away. However, I later discovered that this was not the case and in fact another Skipper would be taking her instead. On speaking with Ray a few years later he told me he had been brought out of the Halifax, putting an experienced Westward Skipper in his place. This turned out to be a disaster with the experienced Skipper losing all the fishing gear aboard the ship, with little or no fish to show for it.

The Skipper who was taking us away, had earned a lot of money deepwater fishing and he would be sailing with his regular Mate, both of whom had never been in a stern trawler. Come sailing day, as usual, I had been summoned to the bridge to steer the ship out of the dock. Quite a few of the deepwater fleet had gone for scrap, others had been sold, to the countries who threw us out of their fishing areas.

Watches were set and I am so pleased that we had been working on the ship for a few days giving me a chance to make a couple of pairs of cod ends prior to sailing. When I had done my jobs, I helped making trawls and small net part, top and lower Wings etc.

We are now forty-eight hours from leaving Grimsby and we had the trawl in the water fishing in the Foula Bank region. We were, fishing with a few Scottish ships, together with a few of Cat boats, Cheetah, Panther etc. Middle water Skippers didn't like passing on information as they had taken years to discover where the best fishing grounds were located. This information was valuable and they did not want to give it away to all and sundry.

Fishing had been quite slack and the Skipper decided to move up the East side of the Shetland Islands. Fishing on various grounds which were new to us, meant that we often became fast but thankfully, only with minor damage. On one haul we developed a problem with the hydraulics and we went into a place called Bslta Sound, tying up alongside a small jetty. I had been called on the bridge to keep an eye out whilst the Skipper and Mate went ashore to see the Agent. They came back after a couple of hours, both under the influence, I might add. Climbing back on board, I was relieved when the Skipper called the crew to the bridge and they were told not to go ashore. I went off the bridge to get my head down whilst I had the chance.

Whilst sleeping I heard plenty for loud noises and voices for what seemed like hours. Being curious, I went to the area were most of the noise was coming from. There were two people on the quayside and they happened to be brothers. The Skipper had been reading the Riot Act to them and words became heated. The Skipper went on the quayside and within minutes he was fighting with one of the crew. Things came to a standstill with both parties being separated by myself and other crew members. A team of hydraulic engineers came and repaired the system and we eventually sailing just after midnight.

The net was soon shot into the water but an hour later we became fast. When we hauled in the net, we had split the trawl in half. With no watch belows on here, we all stayed up to repair the net. The Skipper called the Mate on to the bridge and told him to take his gear off and then told us to carry on with the net. We are changing location and are off to ROCKALL.

From just after breakfast until mid-afternoon we had been mending the nets. Just after lunch we were called for our bond. The usual swag, baccy, fags, soap, sweets and I had been issued with a case of long-life ale. On receiving my case I was told not to get pissed and I was then offered a dram of rum which I refused. I had my own reasons for not taking the long-life.

The trawl had been repaired. We were all told to roll in as the Skipper and Mate would be taking the watches. I stayed up until teatime and had something to eat and soon rolled in as I am feeling dog tired. Just after midnight I had been called out to take the watch relieving the Mate who was half cut. He told me to call him at 0400 hours and we should reach our destination by mid-morning. Things went as planned and I turned in just after 0400 hours and had a few hours' sleep. I was called out just before 1100 hours to shoot the net.

First, we attached the out-hauler hook into the cod ends releasing the net. We then put the out hauler into the bobbin chain which in turn had been released, allowing the rest of the trawl to pull outboard. Soon the dhan lenos followed with chain links to the trawl doors which when attached the doors taken off their chains. They were soon lowered to the required depth. We did this operation for just over a week. We grabbed an hours' sleep here and there when it became available.

The type of fish we were catching was chat haddocks. We had a trip of about 800 kit which were nearly all chats. Some were gutted but mostly rounders [ungutted]. We didn't earn much and just picked up a few pounds with a fry of fish.

The next trip the Mate took her away and Garry Evans came Mate. It's not something that I want to write about as we didn't catch much fish again. I was just happy to get off the ship putting it down to just a bad experience. When we arrived in dock, we were all told that the ship would not be sailing again. On leaving Boston's offices, with my tickets and P45 in hand and feeling very low, I heard my name being called. I quickly turned around and someone that I knew approached me. It was Charlie Ward and he said that I can sign on the Vivaria which will be sailing next week.

3

Vivaria

I HAVE JUST BEEN DOWN DOCK TO SIGN ON!

I have taken a walk around the ship. The watchman let me on when I told him I was the new bosun. He showed me to my cabin and gave me a quick tour around the ship. It seemed strange with no lights on. Creepy, if I'm honest. I thought the Concord had been a big ship until I looked around the Vivaria. I now have a butterfly stomach. I ask myself; 'Have I made the right decision?' I don't think that I know any of the crew!

Well let's see, I have the confidence and I've been taught well by my father-in-law, Bill Ferrand! I had been upset with him when he sacked me and although I understand his reasoning. I've never been SACKED again, as thirdhand!

That time has come again with today, being the last night in dock and as usual we have been to say our goodbyes to both the in-laws and the outlaws. It never gets any easier. If anything, it seems to get harder every trip, especially with the children now growing up quickly. The things we miss, birthdays, school events and most of all being with the family. I don't think that I'm on my own when I say that I never liked the last day at home, especially saying GOODBYE! I don't think that I will get much sleep. I am on edge about sailing as I don't know any of the crew but I will settle down after the first day and just get on with the job in hand.

I was picked up this morning at 0900 hours and back home by 1300 hours because we had a job in the engine room. We are now ordered for 1000 hours tomorrow. When I joined, I was quite happy as I know a few of the crew. I went to Nautical College with the Mate, John Harper and a few of the lads use the same pub as me.

The Skipper welcomed me aboard and I am now looking forward to sailing in the morning. Just popping in the Humber and later the Clee Park before I go home and surprise the wife and kids!

The next day the taxi picked me up just after 1000 hours and I was taken down dock. It was a nice change from being driven all-round the town. I arrived on the dock with a few more bits from home and climbed up the wooden ladders onto the whaleback. I wonder whether Health & Safety would allow this to happen nowadays – I doubt it.

I popped aft and into the galley for a mug of tea and onward into my cabin. The Mate came to see me (John Harper) and gave me the lowdown on who the crew were and who my watchmates would be. One of the men I knew well, Tom Fisher and I always thought of him as a brother to me. The other watchmate was Don Ward, who was the brother of the ship's runner, Charlie. I really felt at ease and looking forward to sailing. The Mate left me going on his travels and within 10 minutes I had been called to the bridge.

The Skipper welcomed me telling me that he had a good crew and that I would soon fit in with them. I was given a quick tour of the bridge with its equipment and I was asked whether I was familiar with the navigation equipment. I told him that I was not. I was shocked at the size of the ship and had not realised how big she was.

The time came and I took my place behind the wheel and was given the various courses and we soon departed the lock pits and headed for the Burcom and onwards to Spurn Lightship. When we were abeam of the Lightship, I was told to put the ships wheel amidships. With a couple of valve changes we are now in Automatic Steering. Both of my watchmates came onto the bridge with the Mate, who told me we will split the first watch, changing mid-afternoon. Now that's music to my ears.

We have just altered course and heading NNE. The rest of the watch went by without any incidents. I gave my handover to the Mate and went below to unpack my gear into my lockers. Whilst I was putting my oilskins, with my duck suit, into the drying room, I had a quick walk around the after quarters and met a few more new faces. I declined the cans and drams being dished out saying; 'Maybe later!'

It had nearly been a waste of time turning in, what with all the different noises and strange rolling motion. I'm sure that I will soon get used to it. Seeing as it is nearly my watch, I took a walk up to the bridge which had three flights of stairs, if I remember this correctly, as it is nearly 50 years ago. My two watchmates soon followed onto the bridge bringing with them a pot of tea.

I kept getting my leg pulled at times by Don but I gave as good as I was given. He remarked that; 'I shouldn't be here as I'm not from this company!' 'I've put one of the regulars out of work.' etc. etc. (I had been in BOSTONS for over 10 years). I replied; 'If your brother wasn't the Ships Runner you wouldn't be in a ship either!' This was only the first day but I soon sorted him out with the same banter. I took the steering out of automatic and put Don on the wheel and after an hour put it back into automatic. The trick worked.

We are about 90 miles from Grimsby with not a single cloud in the sky and for miles we could see the loom of the OIL Platforms in the distance. Shooting stars were in abundance. Watching them burn into the nights atmosphere and wander were the remains landed. Passing plenty of shipping going about their business. I keep getting startled on the bridge as the occasional seagull passed, as they seem to peer into the bridge windows, as they glide by without any effort.

Midnight soon approached when it was time to fill in the log book with a position from the navigation machine, DECCA mark 21, wind speed and direction. This was followed by filling in the Radio Log, 2182 being the channel, distress and weather warnings. We only do the log until the Radio Operator comes on watch and then it is over to him. The time flew by as we were listening to radio Luxembourg until about 0200 hours. The signal would then fade away and it was time to turn the radio off. Just before 0300 hours I put the position on the chart and the Mate came up to relieve me. I handed over the watch and asked the Mate to call me after breakfast so that I could give the dayman a hand. I soon fell asleep this time.

After a hearty breakfast, I'm looking forward to spending some time on the deck to get myself familiarised with the working areas and equipment on hand. The first thing on the agenda was to put the fish washer up along with the deck boards in place. Everything had been going so well, when, whilst the washer had been lifted off the deck, about six feet of big black smoke appeared from the engine room ventilators. A piston ring on the winch had failed which then stopped the winch movements. I am so pleased that the weather had been ok. We managed to put the washer in situ using mainly man power.

After a couple of hours things returned to normal. The Skipper took the opportunity to dish out the Bond and I was one of the first into the Skippers cabin to receive tobacco, a carton of smokes, a tin of quality street, tea and Libby's tinned milk, (evaporated). I was given a case of beer and then given a tot of rum (the measure was a Colman's mustard jar). I downed it in one go. I thanked the Skipper and vacated his cabin, taking my issue to my cabin. Whilst passing people waiting for their issue, I overheard a certain crew member give a snide remark, saying; 'Why has he got a case when we only get 6 cans?' I turned round and said: 'I can be trusted. Can you?' YES, you guessed it. The comment came from an engineer, who I previously had a few choice words between ourselves. To me it was history we had together whilst ashore. To cut a long story we were in the Dolphin Disco and I bopped him at that time. Will I do the same at it at sea, I wonder?

After lunch I went on watch and by 1300 hours, I was back on the deck again. I had just checked all the spare gear and where it was all kept. It's no good sending someone off the deck to get something we need not knowing where things are kept myself.

Mid-afternoon I had been called to the bridge as the Mast Head Light had gone out. Apparently, it was my task to correct the fault and I was given a small shifting spanner and two bulbs. I was informed that the power had been isolated. I thought: 'That's all I need, the electrics on and being 30 feet aloft.' A day man kept an eye on me whilst I climbed slowly up the ladders. I had no safety harness and was just gripping on by my hands. Half way up my legs began to move like Elvis. Reaching the lamp my legs became normal and I slowly undid the top, placed my hand inside and with half a turn I removed the old bulb. I placed this in my pocket and took the new bulb and placed it inside. I shouted to my lookout, who in turn informed the bridge to put the power back on. Hooray, the light came on! I started my descent of the ladders. Once down my legs started shaking again. I called onto the bridge to take my gear off and I could take over my watch again but not before I was given a dram and a thank you from the Skipper.

I had only known the Skipper a matter of days. ROY KURZ, what a gentleman and I soon found out, a clever fisherman. As the Skipper left the bridge, he said: 'Those ships ahead, don't move for them, they will move for you.' There must have been nearly a hundred fishing boats and they had been the Russian Herring fleet. The Skipper was right and true to his word as the ships let me through without having to alter course for anyone.

After a good sleep I took the early morning watch. We had a great show with the Northern Lights. Those of you who have never seen them, you must put it on your bucket list. We just took it for granted.

We have just past Svino which is a landmark in Norway and with the weather being good we are going around the land instead of going through the fjords. We have passed a few local boats, mostly line fishing, with gear that spread for miles. Breakfast soon came upon us and John Harper (Mate) relieved me. I asked if he needed me on the deck and his answer was no. So, with a nice breakfast I retreated to my cabin, taking some clean gear out with the intentions of grabbing a shower when I turned too.

FINALLY, YES FINALLY, we have reached the fishing grounds and we are now at the North Cape. A few Grimsby and Hull trawlers are in this area and reports are saying 50/60 kits for a three-hour tow. Let's get the gear over soon and let us settle down again. The order came just after lunch to standby to shoot the nets with all hands, at this time, to put the gear over the side.

First the otter boards were put over and secured by chain links. Next went the cod ends, soon followed by the bobbins and headline cans, next the dan lenos lowered into the water which were quickly followed by the trawl doors. Speed was gained now, the warps from the winch were being slackened off using the brakes only. Soon the right amount of warp had been used. The brakes were tightened and a messenger hook connected to a wire which had been put on the fore warp which in turn pulled the after warp into the towing block. A pin secured the operation with the verbal scream came: 'ALL SQUARE AFT!' Closed all scupper doors as we are now on the fishing grounds and this is where the fish will be contained.

The Mate had been called onto the bridge for the rum issue which went down a treat when it was dished out. The watches were set with the afternoon being my time on. I was not needed on the bridge as the Skipper wanted to take the tow. I took off my wet gear, with time in the mess deck beckoning for a game of cards. After an hour or so I was called to the bridge with the news that both Russia and Norway are also following Iceland and setting their own 200-mile fishing limits. This means that we have about 12 days to catch a trip.

What on earth will we do if we have nowhere to fish. It's either going to be Midwater Fishing or travelling to Lowestoft to work on Standby boats. **Things are looking GRIM in GRIMSBY.**

Over the last couple of days, we have been averaging 300 baskets of fish a day which is about 160 kits. I must admit the deck crew are a good set of lads. Very quick at gutting the fish and the once or twice that the nets been broken it has quickly been repaired. The crew have been here a couple of years or more and I seem to have fitted right in with them quite quickly. We had a moan about being thrown out of Norway but until we are, we must stay focused on job in hand.

The Northern Lights have given us a fantastic display over the last few nights. I am wondering whether we will ever see them again and the answer is yes. Just after lunchtime we came fast with the net being stuck on the sea bed. Heaving slowly on the winch, when suddenly we became free. Things don't look good with not much weight on the fore warp. It became apparent that we had parted something but WHAT!

Slowly but surely, both the trawl doors came up and we soon discovered that there was plenty of weight on the bridles (cables in Hull) as the dhan lenos appeared. The forward headline had parted, with the top wing being taken out, (lost net). We commenced pulling in the trawl by hand, until we could push the net together and we then let the winch do its job. After about ten minutes we had heaved in the Cod Ends which contained about 60 baskets of large Cod. A couple of the crew were deployed to get a new top wing which had been made up earlier. These are the jobs we do if we get any spare time making top and lower wings, lines of cans (floatation on the Headlines). We always have a spare pair of Cod Ends fully made up as it just saves time whilst on the fishing grounds. What we use we will make up again. Soon the broken net had been replaced, with a new headline wire which had caused the trouble. Now the net was ready to put over again. It had taken us nearly an hour until we were ready to shoot the trawl again. Mind you, the weather had been calm and we were just tying the Cod ends when we had a whiff of fresh bread or pastry coming from the galley. Soon the net was over the side and we are now towing the trawl again. I was called to the bridge to take the Rum round for the morning issue. After taking it around to the crew I returned to the bridge and was given an extra dram for my efforts whilst in charge of the deck, as the mate was watch below from brekkie until dinnertime.

I felt quite pleased with myself. When I went into the fish pounds, I told the crew that I received an extra dram. A few murmurs I heard saying that the Skipper ROY KURZ, didn't let the other Bosun's have extra. Maybe I'm the SPECIAL ONE - AH AH!!

After a couple of days fishing, we have been catching plenty of large cod but now we have been Hampered with small boats using lines stretching for miles. We have been told to move to another area which we did. Talk about being bullied. Twenty-four hours later we had caught 200 kits, when from out of the bridge windows the Skipper called me onto the bridge. Of course, me being me, all the time I was thinking that I done something wrong. Sometimes I was naive, believing I had but not on this occasion. The Skipper passed me a telegram confirming that we are were no longer allowed to catch fish in the Norwegian sector. Angry is not the word I would choose to express how I felt. Deeply upset and feeling let-down by the Government of the day.

Just after lunchtime orders were: given 'Drop the doors in, were going Home!' Usually, when this order was given, everyone would be in 'high spirits' but not on this occasion. When the net came in, we had nearly 100 baskets of cod in the net which was so, so frustrating. The rest of the trawl had been lifted in-board, otter boards, dhan lenos secured. Time for a quick cuppa aft then into the pounds to clean the fish and you could have heard a pin drop. In contrast, at breakfast time, there had an abundance of laughter. It just goes to show how quickly things can change. We are about 60 miles from Honninsvag where we are heading to pick up the pilots. We passed through the fjords, through the North Sea heading for Grimsby.

At the trips end we called into Honninsvag for a couple of hours, fuelled after breakfast and collected a few supplies needed by the cook. The lads took the opportunity to shower and stretch their legs. Kore, the agent, came aboard with the usual storm lighters and a bonus, by giving us a knife each. The pilots came aboard during the afternoon and just before teatime we sailed. Both pilots were delighted that they were given fried fish for tea whilst we had our traditional tasty meals that we came to enjoy on a regular basis. It was my first watch after tea, chatting to the pilots to make small talk, asking me what will I do if and when we dock and what type of work will I do. I couldn't really answer that with Grimsby being the BIGGEST Fishing port in the WORLD nearly all work involved in FISH. I just don't know as I had never really thought about it. To this day, I still take a day at a time. What will be, will be.

Soon the Watch came to an end and I handed the watch over to the mate, John Harper. Like me and most of the crew who had young families, we often talked together with the odd game of Crib or Two. Breakfast time next day I gave the dayman a hand to clear the deck boards, clean the nets out of the old fish etc. and often looking shoreside and seeing in the distance plenty of Reindeer. Remembering the times when we had to lay at anchor whilst they crossed the fjords on their Migratory Challenges. Over the next thirty-six hours having passed through Tromso which I had the privilege in hand steering, taking the ship under the Bridge which turned out to be the last time seeing it.

When night time came we had the grand displays, on clear nights shooting stars as well with the Northern Lights which I have seen in later times. Passing through the North Sea more and more rigs had been appearing with new built oil platforms. They needed crews to ward off ships as well. They were also there in case of events known as standby vessels. I don't really fancy doing that type of work but if needs be, then I will turn my hand to doing it if it pays the bills.

We were soon in the river Humber and eventually sailed through the lock gates. Just tying up alongside the pontoon after our final voyage and all the crews were told to take all their gear off as she won't be sailing again. Unless it has happened to you it is impossible to imagine the feeling of come into dock to be told, you're OUT of WORK with no prospects of continuing your livelihood.

Back in dock, putting my gear ashore the wife had met me and this saved me picking my gear up at a later date. I left all my bedding and deck gear which I didn't need. The crew said their farewells and we went our separate ways. The next day, which was landing day, I was pleased that we had made a decent trip. I collected my money from the cashiers, which was written in pencil which was not the norm. I had never had it written this way before.

I was just passing the runners office when I was pulled aside by Charlie Ward and was told that most of the crew would be sailing in just over a weeks' time in the Ross Kelvin and that Roy Kurz would be taking her. Can you Imagine the RELIEF that this news had been? From that date I had another seven years fishing. But hey. THAT'S ANOTHER STORY!!

A Random Memory

Steaming down to the fishing grounds on a Sunday. Remember being called out for lunch and watch time. Bonzo was the Skipper and he didn't mind me having my meals in the MESSDECK with the lads. He understood that I had been happier eating with the lads. Budgie had been the cook and he was a decent chef with mainly basic meals. He was a good storyteller and we sat down to a lovely roast dinner with all the trimmings, mashed spuds, carrots, cauliflower florets with a thick onion sauce. This was followed by a plain duff for main or sweet course, I had it for my main.

At 1230 hours I went on watch and I didn't have to go on the deck as I had been out from 0800 hours. We were overhauling the cod ends, renewing any cowhides which were needed and finally putting new cod line meshes on the trawl. As we finished putting a new cod line in, one of my watchmates who had been the fish room man was needed to prepare things before we reached the fishing grounds. It was midsummer and the sky had few clouds but just beyond the Horizon we could just see grey masses which we knew were the Faroe Islands. Within the next eighteen hours or so we should be on the grounds searching once more for a decent catch of fish.

Bonzo stayed on the bridge for a while chatting about different topics. I had sailed a few times with him when he was mate. Once on the Belgaum, I had been deckie then, we had been on a fish shop with Tommy Whitcombe, double bagging it. This term is used when we have more than one cod end filled with fish. The second bag of fish came aboard with about 60 baskets of fish and I put the tackle into the halving becket which came away from the bag ropes. Unbeknown to me the hook came out and hit me just above my right eye. Blood soon covering my face. However, I still managed to put the tackle hook into the becket and this time it remained in place which allowed us get the fish onboard. I went aft, took my gear off whilst Bonzo stitched my eye up. I still have the scar but it is now hardly noticeable. Once I was stitched up, I was straight back on the deck to carry on as normal.

Meanwhile back on the Concord the evening meal soon came upon us, usual stuff, known as a Board of Trade Meal. This consisted of cold cuts of meat (ham or beef from lunchtime) salad or chips, fresh busters with BUTTER. The rest of the week it was mainly echo margarine. This was followed by jelly and tinned fruit salad, drizzled with evaporated milk, in which we dipped our bread. I always tried to pinch all the cherries.

Oh, such Happy Memories which should never be forgotten. All for the price of FISH.

4

Ross Kelvin

Will be joining the Kelvin after the Weekend. We are going to be working by her for a week or so, as we are changing her fishing gear from deep-water to middle-water gear. Most of the crew have come from the Vivaria - Wayne Vincent, Dave Pratt, Tom Fisher. The mate, John Harper, is still missing and nobody has seen him since we docked last trip. We now have Jim Trigunna. I'm sure things will feel strange at first. On the plus side we will have shorter trips to do.

We will hopefully be working alongside some great trawler Skippers, the likes of: Dennis Avery, Billy Salt, Paddy

McCarthy, Ronnie Reeves, (JP) Jack Piggott, Dennis Loveday, Wally Stokes, Dennis Speck to name but a few.

It breaks your heart watching the fine fishing boat being taken away to the scrap yards in Europe and home waters. Ships such as the Northern Queen, Prince, Princess, Northern Isles, not forgetting, Everton, Arsenal, Grimsby Town etc, a few of Boston's ships are being converted to Oil and Gas Standby boats and being given a new lease of life, but others have not and are being scrapped. The remaining ships on the North Wall await their destiny.

We've had another full day down dock, bobbins rigged, new trawls made up. My job is to make pairs of cod ends, for starters. A couple of the lads are helping me which is appreciated as it makes things easier for me. The crew seem to be bonding together. No moaning, just getting on with things. The Skipper's was at the Bonded Stores prior to going away and asked if we had any preference as to what we wanted. Six cases of beer each had been suggested complete with a rum or two. The Mate just came down for a visit. He had had a few drinks and was slurring his words saying; 'Are you lot sure you know what you are doing?' The hairs on the back on my neck came up. I took him aside saying come and see us tomorrow. Just after lunch we stopped and finished just after 1400 hours. We called it a day, well, I did, as I'm in charge and am pleased with what we had achieved today. Popped into the Clee Park and just had a couple, then home before tea and a long soak in the bath.

The new Mate, Jim Trigunna, introduced himself during the morning but by mid-afternoon he was taken off us to sail with my father-in-law (Bill Ferrand). Now we have ended up with 'killer' Cook. I've known 'killer' since using the

Corporation and I always got on with him as a friend. Let's see if we get on at sea.

We have only one more day to go before we are ready to sail. Most of the crews' gear is onboard. After lunch she was been moved to get ice for the fish room and the fuel barge gave us the fuel. The food stores, water tanks topped up both being put on in the morning, prior to sailing. As we were about to leave the ship, we were told we have an extra day in dock and with another bonus that we can collect extra money for working by her. So instead of staying in tonight, it calls for a night out in Cleethorpes.

Sailed this morning at 0300 hours and was picked up at 0130 hours with the usual proceedings. It always hurts saying goodbye to the wife and children and it doesn't get any easier. Climbing up the ladder, onto the Whaleback, early morning with my kit bag over the shoulder, walking towards my cabin, meeting some of the crew and newer members whom I had not sailed with before. We have a crew of 14 and hopefully in 14 days we will come home with a decent catch of fish.

I placed my gear in my cabin which I shared with the cook and I was given the bottom bunk. This is when it hits you, from being deep-water having your own cabin and sink. Privacy is limited but we knuckled down to things and adapted to our new surroundings. These ships are not built for comfort, they are work horses. We come on board, do what we have to and go home. Many a ship has not returned; such is the danger of our occupation.

I've been summoned to the Bridge for sailing and take up my position behind the ships wheel; the various courses being steered are various until we came out of the lock pits. Passing channel marker buoys and soon rounding the lightship. The course is set North half West heading towards Flamborough Head. The mate came up with his watch mates taking over the watch, relieving me until my next watch which was lunchtime. Proceeded towards my cabin, refusing a drink for now. Sleep beckoned me so I turned in. Sleep came instantly.

Called out just before lunch for watcho. Both of my watchmates didn't seem happy being on watch [Tommy Fisher and Titch Wescott]. It could have been worse if we were hand steering but we have automatic steering which makes life easier. I have been told to get the dayman out for an hour this afternoon. I'm glad that I'm not the one calling them out. A few curses will be aimed at me but this has come from the mate who turned in just before 1400 hours. One of the daymen came up and said; 'Are you kidding me?' I told him in no uncertain words to 'piss off' - don't come moaning to me, go see the Mate or Skipper.

The weather is kind so just told him to put the washer up and deck boards, then to call it a day. There had been a few ships knocking about so I sent Tommy on the deck to give a hand whilst I navigated through the shipping areas. I ran down the engine room to start the winch. Soon the washer had been lifted into place. The water hose was fitted, just before 1600 hours all the boards and gratings were put into place. All done without any moaning.

Teatime soon approached and I had been relieved by the deckies watch. The mate sat at the table speaking in a loud voice and told me; 'You didn't call the daymen out, did you?'. 'No Comment' - came the reply, laughing at me with tongue in cheek. This time tomorrow we should reach the fishing grounds. Let's hope we can drag a trip out. I thanked the cook for the meal George Nicholson, (Nicho) then turned in for the night. Back on watch 0300 hours.

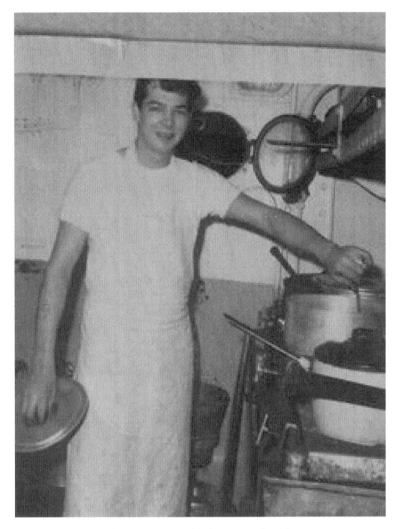

George Nicholson – Cook

Passed Peterhead and Rattary Head just after breakfast. Mid-morning the Bond had been dished out. The weather was a bit fresh after passing Duncansby Head and we had passed through Papa Westray. After lunch fishing watches were set. The Skipper had been trying to get some information from the Cat boats but no one was giving any information. Ross Kashmir had sailed with us and if I remember rightly John Meadows had been Skipper, (correct me if I'm wrong).

Just after 1400 hours we were nearing Foula with quite a few Vessels working in the Area. We were informed to get things ready for shooting the trawl. The doors were hung over the side and all the lashings' chains were taken off the nets. By 1430 hours the ship had eased in speed, with the engines given a kick astern, we came to a standstill. With the order given to heave the Cod ends out, then let go, the net began to pull out. Bobbins went over the rail, followed by the headline with its numerous aluminium floats. The net was lowered into the water, soon followed with the lowering of the doors. Speed had soon gathered when the warps were being payed away, with both warps into the towing block with the order once more: 'ALL SQUARE AFT!' The winchman stood by till the breaks had cooled down before finally putting more pressure on the brakes, if needed.

The Cod Line

Whilst in the drying room I was just about to take my oilskins off when I heard the screeching of the brakes. I was putting my gear back on when things went quiet on deck. The engines had been stopped and the order came to knockout aft (hauling nets). I was just about to go on deck when one of the lads passed me a mug of tea and a smoke (rollie). I thanked the person and I took my place near the winch. We were now turning slowly back over our fishing gear at slow speed and when the obstacle on the seabed became free, the short mark came on board (last 25 fathoms).

We were told to stop heaving on the winch whilst the skipper took a turn out of her by going to starboard. Soon we were told to commence heaving once more. The after door came up and was put on to the dog chain whilst the bridles were unclipped from the trawl door. Soon the fore door came up and the same procedure had to be carried out. No sooner had we started to heave on the bridles (cables) when without any warning the Cod ends surfaced, bringing lots of bubbles as the bellies displayed the catch. We were then told to heave slowly on the winch with the large number of fish.

The Dhan lenos appeared and the brakes were then applied on the winch. The bobbins soon came on the deck, quickly followed by the headline. All hands working in unison started pulling in the net, all the time looking for any damage. Slowly but surely the net came in where we could put beckets on the net. Using the fanny (lifting wire) we were then able to go astern and start lifting the fish out of the nets. Soon the first lift came in with about 50 baskets of the biggest coley that I have seen for a while. We called them torpedoes. In total we did five turns going astern, filling the cod ends, then lifting them in again. We had caught approximately 250 baskets for a 10-minute tow. With no damage to the net, we put it back over the side. No other ship in the area caught any great amounts. That's if they were telling the truth! Payed the net away and soon we were towing the net once more.

I was called onto the bridge to take a Rum issue round. I must have been out of condition as I had been sweating when I reached the bridge. The Skipper told me to take some deep breaths. The adrenaline was sky high as it's a great feeling, seeing a deck load of fish such as we had on deck at that time. Eventually, I dished the Rum out and returned the bottle and dram glass to the Skipper. I had a quick smoke and proceeded to the fish pounds, to gut the fish. After nearly two hours of gutting, with nearly half the fish cleaned, a voice came from aft. 'TEA O!' It had been the cook. I left the deck with most of the lads, whist my two watchmates stayed gutting. I just took my gear off when I passed the Mate and he asked what was happening. I told him that we had caught about 250 bask of large Coley and he gruntled. As I passed him, I told him, you will see for yourself soon enough. I can tell you what though, I've only been on the bridge for ten minutes when I started aching in my arms and shoulders. This is only day ONE!

For your information...

The Art to Gutting a Fish

Pick the fish up in your left hand by holding its gills. With your right hand, holding your knife firmly, cut across the nape. From the nape to the bum hole cut the fish skin wide open, lift out the livers and throw them into a basket. When in season, remove the roe. Cut across the fish's belly, removing all the innards, remove the heart and clots and then throw the whole fish into the washer. Continue doing this until all the fish on deck has been gutted, washed and put in the fish room.

Gutting Fish

Over the last couple of days, we have averaged about 70 kits of fish a day. No other ships had caught any amount of coley. We must have been in the right place at the right time. Things are getting easier with the Cat Boat Skippers' as they seem to be giving more information about different areas. A few ships are on the Papa Bank catching a few cod on short tows. We are going to the Big Hammer, as apparently plenty of fish is being caught as well or if there is no fish a lot of damage could be done. Let's see! Getting on with 'killer' Cook - by he can tell a yarn or two. He was a very good net mender and I am learning a lot from him, for example, how to look at the net and see if any is missing etc. I always remember the size of his hands, pulling on the net effortlessly. He was as strong as an ox.

It is nearly mid-morning; the nets have been lowered and we are now towing the gear behind us. I have been told it will be only a short tow which in fact it had only been an hour. When the net came up half the belly had been ripped out. We were told to lace it together for now. The next haul had fifty baskets of large cod and with no damage this time. We were told to lift the doors as we will be steaming for an hour or so to Esha Ness as reports are saying that the fishing is a lot better at this location. We took to the fish pounds, clearing the fish away in the pounds, when suddenly thick black smoke appeared.

Looking aft as the black smoke appearing on deck, the crew and I ventured aft. The Fire Alarms were blaring out, ringing off the bells. The cook [Nikko] appeared on the deck saying that he had left a pan of chips inside the oven and forgot about them, whilst he grabbed an hour in his bunk. The cook worked long hours, with most getting up at 0430 hours to quickly make a batch of busters (bread buns), in time for breakfast which usually consisted of a full English whilst supplies endured which lasted for about a week or so. We had cereals, porridge etc with tinned milk, kippers and smoke fish and of course we had fresh fish that had been on the ice. When the Skipper found out what had happened, he gave Nikko a right Rollocking.

Thinking about it later it could have had severe consequences as we [the crew] would not have been able to reach our lifejackets which were in our cabins. Speaking to Nikko, later on in years, he just laughed it off and said that he wouldn't be the only cook to let this happen.

After checking that everything had been ok, we went back into the pounds. We had just settled down to gutting the fish, standing in the pounds, merrily gutting away, when a shout came from the Bridge Window that we are hauling our nets. Along the portside an inflatable appeared with three men boarding the ship. These men were from the Fishery Protection Ship HMS Guernsey who wanted to inspect the nets. One man went straight to the Bridge, with the other two standing forward.

Bringing In The Cod End

We started to bring the gear up, doors, Dhan leno etc. and we started pulling the net in until finally the cod ends came on board. The two men observing forward, started measuring the mesh sizes and the size of fish. After completion of the net inspection, they checked the fish hold. Finally, they checked the net store. The man on the bridge came down and told us to give them a basket of mixed fish, which went into the inflatable returning to the HMS Guernsey. There were various international vessels near us but did they inspect them, of course not. If they had, they would have found infringements with their gear, which would have caused an international incident. It was always the case that they would inspect any local ships but would they search foreign ships – NO!!!

HMS Guernsey - A Fishery Protection Ship

We have been fishing now for just over a week, ten days to be exact and this will be our last haul of the trip coming up. Yesterday had been another tough day because, just after breakfast, we became fast. It took us nearly three hours to haul the net as it was full of Dog fish. It had been very difficult to pull the net manually and we had to use a rope named a Snorkeler. We pulled the net, as much as we could and threaded the rope through the ships outside rail. We then tied a bowline in the rope and lowered it as much as we could, slowly but surely, after about a dozen times we heaved the mass weight to the ships rail. The Skipper went astern. Luckily the halving becket extension rope floated to the surface, using the gaff. (Long pole with a hook at the end). We were able to put the Gilson Wire, then Tackle (double purchase lifting block) we were able to bring the full net inboard together. It rolled over the side with about thirty feet of net full of dog fish. We then steamed towards Sum Burgh whilst we cleared the net of fish.

I can't tell you how many times that the sharp hooks on the back of the fish cut my hands, as well as the rest of the crews. Not an easy task to empty the nets but we just got on with it until we completed the task. Just after lunch the nets were clear, and the fish was being put away, which took in total nearly three hours. We don't gut the dogfish and just threw them down the fish room whole. We had a few holes in the nets which we mended and by about 1530 hours we were towing again, hopefully away from the Dogfish! I know one thing - I will sleep tonight!

'Drop the doors in!' came the order from the Bridge. 'We're going HOME!' Laughter and cheering soon came from the deck crew. The mate is watch below and missed crewing up again. We have hauled with about 40 baskets of mixed fish which has been an average catch each haul. We have stowed most of the net and lashed the bobbins down using chains as the weather forecast is not in our favour, with a south westerly 6 to 8 predicted.

I was called the bridge to take the final rum issue around, with a few moans being chanted as I told the lads, soon after we were gutting the fish with a fine spray now coming over the whaleback. Soon after the gutting had been completed, we began to dismantle the fish pounds and the gratings. We put away the washer, the shoot had been taken away, then the washer had been taken down. We were using lashings to stop it swinging. We soon had it under control and secured alongside the port spare doors. The men down the fish room came out of the hatch just as we were leaving the deck. How strange!

I was just about to leave the deck when the Skipper shouted; 'Lift all the scupper doors.' This was a precaution, just in case we got any amount of water on the decks, meaning it would soon clear. All hands safely inside the ship when the engine gathered speed. WE ARE GOING HOME. The trip will be 15 days, dock to dock with 850 kits of fish. Bit of all sorts but we should make some money for our efforts at SEA.

Taking my sea gear off in the drying room, we soon felt the ships bow dipping and weaving as we gathered speed. A quick pot of tea in my hand, my watchmates and I soon ventured on the bridge to take the first watch. It's now 0200 hours only four more hours to go. I am suddenly feeling very tired and all we want to do is to go home spend time with the family and in a few days' time we will be sailing again!

With the same routine of getting picked up in a taxi and being dropped off alongside a ship. Walking up a ladder, over the whaleback and down to your berth. Putting your personal items away then awaiting orders to sail. The, Mate appears and barks his orders, telling you what you will be doing, either a watchkeeper or a dayman. As soon as he disappears the drams and the cans come out. Most times we didn't sail for nearly two hours, so a few cans and drams were often consumed. The Mate often returned to the after focsal and he joins the party mood. This voyage I've been picked as a daymen which I enjoyed more than being a watchkeeper. Orders to let go came from the bridge and we all take up our positions to sail. As we are leaving the dock the yoyo is set up and the fish washer put into place. We are then all ordered off deck but not before all watertight doors and scuppers are secured. The party berth carries on and the spoons come out with the sing-songs. Gradually the men turn in. Next day the daymen are called and some are feeling rough with a few 'Huey's and Ralphs' but eventually things turn to NORMALITY.

After a couple of days doing the same thing, we reach the grounds with nearly two weeks of fishing time. Standing in the fish pounds in all sorts of weather, rain, wind, sleet, snow, and often freezing conditions, we went through the same procedure daily. Having cold hands with often runny noses which you tried to remove in any fashion. Standing waist deep in fish or waist deep mending the nets, we worked eighteen hours a day, sometimes more if we had to chop ice. We did complain to ourselves, ('this is my last trip' was often heard) but we always sailed again. Hopefully returning with a good catch of fish and make a good market but we are always grateful that we have returned safely home where sadly others have not.

I have just been down dock to discover that most of the deep-water vessels have now been taken away to be scrapped, with a few being sold to Norway, Iceland and Russia. It just seems strange seeing the docks empty of ships. A few Boston ships have been taken to Lowestoft (Colne Shipping) as they are being converted to oil and gas support vessels. A couple of CONSOL ships have net drums and continued fishing for mackerel and herring fishing. Boston had three pocket stern trawlers named Shawnee, Mohave and Sioux with some of Boston's Skippers. I had been offered a job in either the fishing or standby but I refused at this time. I noticed on the slipway, my next ship, Ross Genet, sitting proudly on the slips and I never realised how big she looked out of water.

The trawler owners laid the Ross Kelvin up as it was costing top much money in fuel.

Lucky me. Ross Genet. Sailing Thursday. Skipper Pete Bartlett.

5

Ross Genet

Usual trend of popping round to see the in-laws and the outlaws before we sail on Thursday. It's more like a ritual but as we all know; strange things happen at sea and I will leave that there.

Before I was married, I lived with my grandmother. She was a good cook and always made tarts and pastries for me and the crew. They would be in a Quality Street tin and I would place the tin in the messdeck and within a couple of hours they had all gone. However, nobody ever admitted to eating them.

On the last night in dock, I would be moody. Thinking to myself 'Shall I tell the taxi on Thursday morning to piss off?' but I never did. Early to bed with it being an early morning pick up. Let's see what happens next.

Up nice and early ordered for 0200 hours. That's the only thing wrong with Grimsby being tidal and being ordered two hours before tide time. After umpteen fags and coffees, the taxi arrived with Bill Seizer knocking at the door. I then went upstairs and said my goodbyes. I could quite happily have jumped back in to bed but with having a family to feed and a mortgage to pay, I had to go. I kissed them all goodbye and told them individually that I loved them. Quickly down the stairs through the front door, then I stopped in my tracks.

On opening the door, with my kitbag in hand, Bill Seizer held the car door open for me to get in the taxi. The problem was it was a funeral hearse that took families to and from to the cemetery. I asked him; 'What's this?' He replied that his car was being serviced and his boss said that he could use this person carrier until his was repaired. The only good thing was that it was the middle of the night and nobody would see me.

Soon, we were on the North Wall joining the ship. I asked when I got on board; 'Where does the bosun sleep?' I was told I would be sharing the cook's cabin but that's when I noticed a spare bunk in the four-man cabin, so I pulled rank and took the bunk. Tommy Fisher and Dave Pratt were some of the crew members who I had sailed with before. Nikko, the cook was sitting on the seat locker when the Mate appeared and when he saw me, he said; 'Oh it's you again!' I'm not going to name him but his first name was Jimmy. I was about to say something or maybe twat him one when I was summoned to the bridge. The Skipper, Pat Philipson, gave me various courses whilst in the dock then we sailed through the lock gates heading towards the Burcom. Forty minutes later we passed Spurn Lightship. The Mate came up with his watchmates and basically told me to 'EFF OFF!' Watch this space, as we head towards the Western Isles.

Eighteen hours out of Grimsby, the bond was issued. The usual stuff, two hundred St Moritz, for the wife, five tins of old friend plus ten packets of fag papers [Rizla], Typhoo tea, large tin of Quality Street [for taking home], two bars of lux soap and finally six cans of coke, plus twelve cans of beer. Making my way down the bridge steps I heard a snide remark from a certain person saying 'Hope that you've left some for me!' I ignored the remark and I went to put my bond away. I had a can of beer to wash down the rum which was issued when the bond was given out.

I sat down for lunch. With Nico the food was always good and he always kept himself clean, although not every chef was as particular. After dinner I went on to the Bridge to take my watch. The Skipper pulled me aside and asked what's happening between me and the Mate. I just said that it was history, when I had sailed with my father-in-law (Bill Ferrand) and I told him that it would soon be sorted. When the Skipper returned from his lunch, he told me I could go on the deck for a couple of hours with the 'Day Girls' which I gladly accepted as the weather was so hot.

Whilst on the deck, in just jeans, boots and tee shirt, working with the lads and overhauling the trawl. The Mate came on the deck and having had a few beers, was once again mouthing off! I cleared out of his way and went under the whaleback just to try and calm down, as I was ready to explode. I'm now down the fore hold checking the spare parts of the net etc. when a pair of feet descended down the ladders. The Mate squared up to me and as he was about to say something I backhanded him twice. He staggered near the net bins and I made my way back on to the deck, as if nothing had happened. The Mate came up soon after and left the deck. I can always remember Tommy Fisher saying; 'Have you twatted him Ron?' I just winked at him and carried on working. Dinner time came and the Mate relieved me. As I handed him the watch, he apologised saying that he had been out of order. I just said; 'Lesson learned!' and quietly left the Bridge.

The moral of the story is '**BULLYING - stop it in the BUD!** The Skipper told to me that I was right and that I had quickly sorted out the problem.

Just before tea we put the trawl over. The watches had been set so let's hope we can catch a decent trip. Relieved the Skipper for his tea, when he returned, I had mine and then went below. Just after midnight called out with fifty baskets of mixed fish which was mostly cod and haddock. The gear was shot away and now it's the Skippers turn, with his two watchmates to go below. Just settled down to gut the fish and we came fast. With the net being released from its obstruction we had lost the forward top wing which we replaced and within the hour we were back into the fish. Two hours later finished gutting the fish. I just got aft when the Mate shouted out, letting us know that we would be hauling in ten minutes. When we hauled not one single fish was caught.

I had a quick check of the cod ends and we put the gear back over. Shot the net away, warps were put in the after block and told it didn't look right as the warps were closed, meaning we were not toeing the net properly. We knocked the warps out of the blocks, started to heave on them, and discovered we had locked the two trawls' doors together. Heaving slowly, we could soon see where the warps were laid. We took the winch out of gear and opened the breaks until the warps went slack. Luckily, we only did it the one time and it cleared itself. We brought the net to the surface and seeing no damage, we tried again. Just after 0400 hours we were all square. A quick tidy up in the galley and mess making sure it was clean and tidy to give the cook a clean start. We don't want to upset the cook.

Just after breakfast we hauled with 10 baskets of rubbish. The Skipper was now up and he called me on the bridge. The orders the Skipper had given to the Mate were simply ignored and he did his own thing. I'm not getting involved in this one.

It never rains but it pours. I went behind the winch to guide on the warps to give the lads a rest (working as a team). Both clutches shipped up on the Winch. The call came to knock out and we started hauling the net, only 200 fathoms of warp out, when the 100 fathom came in and noticed a couple of strands had gone in the fore warp (lock doors early morning).

I shouted up to the bridge to let the old man know the situation. The trawl came up with 50 baskets of mixed fish with no damage to the net. We were told to pull the warp off and check it. It soon became apparent that it needed repairing. I was told to chop the bad warp out and splice the warp together. I had never done this before, so here goes. I chopped two fathoms out, tied the two parts together with six-foot ends, tied both sides down with a hatch batten and started to take the turns out to open up the warp. Luckily, I had Johnny Walker holding the batten, with Tommy Fisher holding the wire strands together. We soon finished one end.

Dinner time was called and with Johnny and Tommy we started doing the other end. The crew who had their dinner and came back on the deck together with the Mate. I presumed that the Mate would relieve me but he just came up to me and said that he couldn't splice and so I carried on and completed the task. Wire ends chopped off; warp heaved back onto the barrel. I then left the deck but not before being called on the bridge to be thanked by the Skipper who gave me a dram of rum. The cook had saved us some dinner and the time was now 2000 hours. With my hands sore, feeling tired and narked, I rolled into my pit.

After 12 days we were ordered home with about 850 kits and we made about £20,000 which was ok.

The Mate got the sack and I was called into the office and was given an extra £20 for doing the splice. The Foreman Rigger approached me saying they usually repaired the warps but the one I had done was the best that he had seen. I'm sure that I gave both Johnny and Tommy a treat.

I never came across the Mate again and something tells me, from my heart, that I'm glad that I didn't.

I'm pleased that my father in-law HELPED me by splicing the old bridles whilst I was with him at sea.

Another Memory

On another occasion, whilst I was on the Genet, we sailed at 0830 hours. The usual stuff driving half way around the town. Oh, how I could thump effing sizer. He is a taxi driver not a ships runner. Him telling me to hurry up because he's running late. Now he can eff off and I told him not to come back for me until I've said my goodbyes to the wife and kids. The part time job that he does is working for an undertaker. I think that he wanted to drop us off then carry on with his other work. Anyway, he did come back 10 minutes later. Now I'm ready to get in the taxi. It had been known that if he came twice on sailing day, he would charge you for two pickups. That's the type of guy we are dealing with.

Well, that's put me in a good mood for sailing and I think I will leave it here till we sail. Popped my head into the galley and there were Tommy Burton (cook) rustling up a pan of shackles and they smelt lovely. I went down below to put my gear away and now I can relax.

I was called to the bridge by the Skipper who radioed the Fish Dock Island asking for permission to sail which was given. The ladders were pulled up from the whaleback and secured to the after-port handrail. Kick a stern 10 degrees, starboard wheel then midships, now heading towards the lock gates and towards open water which was the River Humber with Burcom and Cleeness soon passed. We are now steering towards Spurn Light Vessel. The Mate came on to the bridge to relieve me and the Skipper pulled rank saying that I would be taking first watch. GUTTED as I didn't get much sleep, well a few hours, as on hearing cars pass down our street, I thought that I had overslept and that the taxi had been outside waiting.

Soon my two watchmates came up, Tommy Fisher and Ploughboy Davis, who had fetched me up a hot cup of coffee which I accepted with thank. It had been the middle of August and the sun had been blazing down, with lots of pleasure craft along with merchant boats running in and out of the estuary. The Skipper told us that we had to go to the Faroe Islands, Torshavn, to pick up a belly and cod ends so that we could fish in their Waters. Soon the Skipper rolled in asking to be called at lunch. This is when I would be going below. Just settling down on watch when the Chief appeared on the Bridge asking for the Skipper. Effing hell, here we go again! Bloody hell, we have sailed without any fuel but enough to get us to Aberdeen. Maybe get a pint or two in the **QUARTERDECK!**

Tied up this afternoon at Blaikie's Quay in Aberdeen. We can't get fuel for another 4 hours. We are berthed alongside the Quarterdeck Public House and Restaurant. It's so, so tempting to go ashore for a quick pint. A couple of lads asked if they could go ashore to stretch their legs and I asked the same. The answer came back; 'Yes, as long as you keep out of the pubs!' So off we went up to Union Street which is massive with all the Major retailers, smart cafes and plenty of public houses. I went into a bakery and asked for some Busters. They looked at me as though I was an alien and gave me something they called a rowie or an Aberdeen roll which was still warm.

Most of us then phoned home to our loved ones whilst we still had the chance. We then made our way back to the ship. A couple more went ashore to stretch their legs ignoring the rules and came back under the weather. Whilst alongside a few of us had a shower and a change of clothes, whilst the engineers topped the tanks up with freshwater. 1900 hours and an oil tanker appeared on the quayside to give us fuel and I was invited ashore for a couple of shandies by the Mate just in the Quarter Deck. People who knew Killer Cooke (only had half a lager) the rest being Rum, with the lager to wash it down. We were sitting in the bar when we heard our ships whistle signalling us to re-join the vessel. Ten minutes later we left the Harbour and are now bound towards Duncansby Head. I'm on watch from 2300 hours until 0300 hours and it's just after midnight. I'm glad I only had a shandy. Passing Peterhead plenty of traffic mostly Supply Boats. As we make our way to Rattary Head the heavens opened up with a fine display of lightening which lit up the sky followed by the rumble of thunder. At sea there are never two days the same. Now we are heading to the NORTHERN WATERS.

I came off watch at 0300 hours and handed the watch over to the Mate who still stank of Rum. There's nothing worse than the stale smell of booze, it's on par with fish. I've just signed off in the log book and radio log. I said my farewells and went down to the messdeck for a sarnie, having looked at what was left of the night's supper. Curled up bread, a piece of spam with teeth marks in, dried up corned beef and a few lettuce leaves and what looked like seeds from tomatoes. I settled for a cup of char and a quick smoke, then rolled in. One of the watches came off the bridge to square the galley up before the cook turned too.

My bunk had been in the four-man cabin on the port quarter alongside the bathroom and changing room. Quite cosy, if truth be told but sometimes noisy when the crews were putting on their work gear. Just before lunch I was called for the bond and had been given twelve cans of Red Bass, the usual smokes of tobacco and cigarettes, a few chocolates, Mars bars and Milky ways, 2 packets of PG Tips with canned milk to make our own special cups of tea. I also made sure that both my watchmates had also acquired some. I soon put my bond away. I then went into the messdeck for tea which consisted of a thick mixed vegetable soup with an onion duff or fresh busters. Me being me, had both. I can still taste that soup which had been outstanding.

We are well clear of the land and should be in Torshavn by breakfast time. It should be earlier but that's the time we have ordered the pilot. It's now mid-afternoon and I've been working on the main deck with the Daymen. The weather has been flat of calm when SUDDENLY a whooshing sound came from the starboard side. Looking over the rail there were about six Orca whales swimming alongside side and pushing on the side of the ship, as if they were scratching their backs. As quickly as they had appeared they disappeared!

I've just been summoned to the bridge, just as we have spotted the Faroese Pilot Launch where we were escorted into Torshavn. I was summoned to the bridge to steer the ship whilst we got alongside. The trip continued without further incident and we didn't see the Orca's again that trip.

Another Random Memory

Yet again, another trip whilst on the Genet the gates are opening. Trawls are all stowed for passage to the Westward. The new Mate has joined the crew and we have just taken her out of the dock, heading for the lightship with a NORTHERLY GALE. Everything has been lashed down with all watertight doors closed. Just passing Bull Fort and we are starting to roll a bit as we slowly steam ahead.

I have the first watch and I'm on the wheel, hand steering. After twenty minutes both my watch mates come up on the bridge Tommy Fisher and Scarborough John, with a mug of strong coffee for me. As we approached the Light Ship, we started diving in to the seas which lifted the bow out of the water. She then came down and the sea lifting her stern up out of the water causing a shuddering all the way through the ship. The Skipper shouted from his cabin to ease her in to half speed which instantly made things a lot calmer. With weather like this lunch would be a pan of shackles which wouldn't go amiss today. I've been quite lucky at sea, sailing with some fine cooks. I really can't remember sailing with bad chefs.

After an hour or so on watch, the Mate came onto the bridge looking concerned, saying that his personal gear was missing from his cabin and asking my watchmates if they had seen it. I told him that I haven't as I had been on the bridge since sailing. He told me that it had definitely been placed in his cabin by himself and it was a suitcase and he told me he had a couple of beers in the focsle. After half an hour or so it had disappeared. We sent one of the lads down to look for it but it didn't turn up. Sometimes we play tricks on lads but this is something else. The Skipper heard the commotion and seeing we were in range of the office he called to arrange for another ship to bring a fresh supply of personal items etc.

The very next day we were sheltering near Dennis Head, unable to put the gear in the water. We were thirty-six hours from sailing and one of Taylors ships sailed bringing the Mate some more gear. When the vessel approached us, stern to stern, we transferred the gear onto us. I was surprised to see that the Skipper had been John Meadows. Taylors had a few middle water vessels, Hondo. Erimo, Osako Okino, Yesso. I am sure that someone will know which ship he had been in.

Being called out at midnight, with two paralytic trawls and a gale of wind, is not an ideal situation to be in. Staggering on the deck as the ship leans into the weather and within five minutes of being on the deck, I have a boot full of water. Stood on the winch grating to empty my boot when I spot the Mate working on the trawl. He told me it needs a new belly top in, with a lower wing in the after end. He then left me to it whilst he relieved the Skipper on the Bridge. The ship was now head to wind and not performing so angrily. As the lads chopped the old belly head out, I stood aft taking the old lower wing out. I had been bent down chopping the twine off the Lancaster's when the ship dipped its rail and filled the deck. I am now effing wet through! The Mate shouted from the bridge to get off the deck for a while whilst we dodged under the Noup Headland.

All hands off the deck now and it is a chance to put some dry clothes on. I emptied my boots in the drain, chucked my wet gear in the sit-up bath, gave it a quick rinse with fresh water and hung it over the bath. I soon put on my fresh gear. After a smoke and hot drink, we were now under the land to finish the mending. By 0300 hours the net was repaired and lashed up for now. The net on the portside had been ripped in a few places but the net had been all there. Just before breakfast the job was completed and the net lashed up. We are now sitting down in the mess having breakfast. When the mate came down off the bridge, I was told to drop the anchor, saying we won't be putting the net over until after lunch, at the earliest. I dropped the anchor with the deckies on my watch. By 0800 hours I was in the land of nod.

I was called out for dinner then onto the bridge for anchor watch. You don't always have days like this and it doesn't always happen as whilst on the bridge the other ships at anchor were all egging each other on to shoot the trawl. Our Skipper said 'It's not worth it and we will put the nets over when the weather is better! 'After a stormy night and morning, the weather abated. Now we are leaving the Noup and heading towards Eshaness were we finished off last trip with a few hauls of jumbo haddocks.

Just before teatime and we are now fishing again, after losing another eighteen hours fishing time. At 2100 hours the nets were hauled with 60 baskets of large haddocks. I had been called at midnight and we caught a similar amount. No other ships were in our area and no information had been passed to other ships. A couple of hauls and we had a few small holes in the net but these were repaired without any lost time.

After a couple of days, the fish took off and we are now fishing around Foula and catching mixed fish. At night we had glimpses of the northern lights and this is when we reminisce about being at Iceland. Do I miss it? Of course, we all do but I'm afraid that's history now and we must never forget our times away, being Distant Water Fisherman.

A week or so later we are now entering the lock gates with nearly 1,000 kits of fish, with a good mix mainly cod and Haddock.

After we landed, I came out of the ship and signed on the Ross Civet, with Kojak. Let's see what transpires next!

6

Ross Civet

Just been down dock today to take my gear of the Ross Genet. She is only two ships apart on the North Wall. As I'm leaving the Genet the Skipper had just pulled up on the quayside and started approaching me. When he was alongside me, he asked why I had come out of the ship. I said that he had taken the Mate out to be replaced by a relative of his whom I didn't like and still don't to this day. Without putting names on paper, he was known to be a bully and you all know my stance with BULLYING. Anyway, I told him it was my choice and my choice alone. Unbeknown to me Tommy Fisher found out I was leaving and signed on the same ship as me. I was then asked; did I want to change my mind. People who know me, know that

I don't go back on my word. We both shook hands and went about our own business.

The Watchman let me on board the Civet asking who I was and I replied; 'the Bosun' and he showed me to my berth. This time I'm sharing with the cook, Pete Bowman, whom I've sailed with before. He always talked about Dolly, his partner, when he had, had a drink or two. The Watchman said that he wouldn't sail across the dock with our skipper and that he used to be an engineer. I soon found out why, it was well known that he did hate ENGINEERS!

I stepped off the ship and was given a lift to the Humber pub. Usual people near the wicket, Harry Scotter Billy Jones, with a few other familiar faces, that I can't recall at this time. Just had a couple of pints, then down to the Corporation. Killer Cook, Big Smithy. Billy Waco, Sid Dillon, Steve Rodger and a few local ladies, Nuf Nuf, Trouser Nell, etc. Had a couple of pints with Tich Wescott who gave me a Mercia pipe which I still have knocking about somewhere. Said my goodbyes then started for home. Not sailing until Friday and now it's time to relax, until we are at sea again. Lots of people told me not to sail with Scotty but I like to decide for myself and will have my own opinion after I've sailed with him.

Ordered for 0300 hours and was picked up at 0330 hours, by the man Sizer. As usual he took us all around the Grange then up to the Nunny. I lived in Daubney Street which was about 5 minutes from the docks. I asked him why he always picked me up first and he reply that I was always ready. For effing sake, it makes me stressed even before we have sailed. The other taxi driver, Snowy, was not much better. By 0415 hours we are now on the North Wall, alongside my new berth for a fortnight or longer. I climbed up the ladders, over the breakwater, down the whaleback ladders, gradually entering the aft accommodation and on into my cabin. I started to put my gear away, when the cook entered and had already started about Dolly.

Jimmy Greene, the Mate rescued me, giving me the low-down of the ship and what to expect from Kojak the Skipper. I didn't need to go in to the stores. I started to use Tiplady's which seemed ok or I could use Gerald Bailys. I didn't like getting robbed by Vincent's or Dobby's and it was my choice again. Just after 0500 hours I was summoned to the Bridge and introduced myself to the Skipper. He shook my hand saying that he had good reports from other Skippers and welcomed me as a new crew member. I thought to myself; 'That's a good start!'.

We sailed without any problems and I was to take the first watch, splitting it with the Mate. I took 3 hours with my watch mates, changing at 0900 hours. My next watch would be at 1830 hours. Coming off watch I had a corned beef sarnie and slice of ham and I then turned in. I had the bottom bunk. Pete was still muttering about Dolly but sleep soon came my way and I was off in the land of Nod. I always felt tired that first day. Now I have to settle down to working long hours, with little sleep. Welcome aboard the CIVET!!

After having a good kip in the afternoon, I was called out and had my tea. It was now time for me to take the evening watch. We have just passed the Farne Islands and are now losing the sight of the land. Not much traffic about and the weather is good, unlike last trip. Soon the watch had passed and it was once more time for some shut-eye.

I was called out for breakfast and settled for a full English. Pete the cook always used plate service, meaning you ordered your food and he passed it through the serving hatch. A few complained but not me as the meal had always been piping hot. Once he knew what you liked and how much food you would eat, he would see who had asked, then serve up.

After breakfast I went on watch and the Skipper sent me down with the daymen. First thing I checked were the cod ends and noticed that a few cod line meshes were broken. I had been told that everything was been ok but I don't always listen to other people and always check these things myself. I cut all the meshes off, put a new set on, put a new cod line in and tied them up but not before checking inside for any holes etc. The cowhides looked ok and so I started helping the lads by lowering the washer in place. The deck boards gratings quickly followed, a couple of the 'daygirls' were hungover working like zombies. They will be like this until they have a livener to see them through the morning.

I went aft for a tea break which lasted about 20 minutes and then the bond was called. I was summoned to the bridge whilst the Skipper issued the bond. I took a pillowcase with me and had been the first in line. The usual stuff, smokes, mars bars, triangular milk (pasteurised) which I kept in a cold locker, (inspection locker to the ships side). I was then given 12 cans of Red Bass and finally a mustard jar full of Rum which went down nicely. I took my bond onto the bridge until we were relieved at 1230 hours. We were just abeam of Buchaness as I signed off the Log and went off the bridge. I placed my Bond in my cabin and was now ordering my lunchtime meal when I heard, in the distance, a cry of. HELP!!

On investigation I discovered one of the crew had fallen down the crew's accommodation ladders and just to make it clear, the person was a non- drinker. I scrambled down the ladder and it looked as though nothing had been broken.

The Mate and myself administered first aid using bandages and pain killers. The Mate suggested that he be put ashore to receive further treatment, as deemed necessary. The Mate went to see the Skipper whilst I had my lunch. Whilst in the messdeck we felt the ship leaning over and knew at once that we had turned around, going southerly.

I had my lunch and I ventured to the bridge where I was informed that the Peterhead lifeboat would take the man off and put him ashore for us. We couldn't go alongside with having the Bond locker open and dished out to the crew. We dodged outside Peterhead Harbour and just before teatime the pilot vessel brought the injured sailor back to us. He was told to rest for a few hours and given some strong painkillers.

Have rest time with KOJAK - you're having a laugh!

I stayed up for tea then went below. We had Beef Wellington with all the trimmings, as it had been the main meal, followed by baked rice pudding, with the skin to die for, sprinkled with cinnamon. With my stomach full of food, I ventured to my cabin. I had a couple of roll ups and then turned in for the night. Just before 2300 hours I had been called out for watch and we were just passing Duncansby Head. We have now set course to go around Dennis Head. I noticed lots of lights in the distance and discovered that they were oil and gas supply boats who support the rigs around the Shetland Islands. At 0300 hours my watch had just been relieved on the bridge. We should be fishing before lunchtime. I am hoping to get a good night's kip!

All hands called out just before breakfast, I was told to leave the Mates watch and now we are on fishing watches which is usually ten days of pure hell. Let's just wait and see what happens. After breakfast both trawl doors were lifted over the ships rail. I went forward to tie the cod line and when completed the cod ends were lifted over the rail. The order came to 'Let Go!' and cod ends fell in the water. Soon the bellies streamed over the side. The bobbins then went over whist we made sure that the quarter ropes were tied down and slip applied. Both hitches were taken off and the order came to knockout the slips which would let the bobbins fall over the side. Quickly, the dhan lenos followed, the ship gathered away and the trawl doors were then lowered. When the depth was reached both door warps came together in the towing block and secured on the after quarter.

Just before lunch we hauled in the net with 60 baskets of large cod and everyone seemed in high spirits. Again, the net was put over and I was summoned to the bridge to dish out the rum issue. When I returned the bottle, it was lunch time, so I stayed on the bridge until the Skipper had his meal and then I went down for mine. In just under two hours the fish had been put away. The person who had been sent down the fish room to help out until he was able to use his hand for gutting was now on deck. 1430 hours and we caught another 40 baskets of the same fish. How lucky are we? No other ships are in this area. HAVE I SPOKEN TOO SOON!

After four days fishing, we have averaged around 150 baskets a day, with little or no mending. We had to change a couple of 21-inch bobbins that had split, filling each time with water. This only took about 20 minutes and we were back in operation. We just had to undo a shackle connection, pull the wire cable manually and replace with new ones. We then heaved on the cable and attach to the shackle connection once more.

During the afternoon we came fast after towing for about two hours. We knocked out the towing block and started to haul the trawl doors up, when up she surfaced. Light blue bubbles then the belly and cod ends spread out. We were told to heave the net in slowly so as not to put any pressure on the net. Eventually the dhan lenos came up and we unhooked the quarter rope links and started heaving on them. When they came to the rail we attached the slips to the quarter links, secured the rope on the cleats, then started to close the net by hand until we had the snorkeler rope wrapped around the net. The ship went astern filling the cod ends up, which was then hauled onto the decks. I untied the cod line, lowered it down on the deck and then released the final locking turn. The fish were now pouring out of the end. The net was then lifted and I retrieved the cod line and retied it, without knotting the ends. I stayed in the fish pounds. The ship went astern again which we did for a total of four times. Finally, the last one came in and I tied the cod line and this time knotted the ends and shot away. No ships were around us and I'm sure that Kojak didn't mention the haul that we had caught.

The fish we caught were mostly extra-large cod with a third being large coley. A few of us had difficulty throwing the fish in the washer so we used Gobby Charlie, the bridge RAT, to make sure they were washed and he threw them down the hatch manually. Not everyone missed the washer, just a couple of the old boys, Carnation George, Tich Wescott, to name a couple who retired shortly after being at sea for a few years. We all have to retire one day, says the man who at 74, doing four tours a day, only for three days a week. This is my choice as I really enjoy reliving life on a trawler.

It had only taken us an hour and a half to get the trawl up, emptied and back in the water. The skipper sent another rum issue, only for the deck crew, the Rat just SMILED at the Skipper. Teatime soon came upon us and we had cleaned about half the catch. I went to bed at 1900 hours and called out at 0200 hours with couple of hours gash time below. We shot the net away at 0300 hours then back into my PIT for a couple more hour's gash. Get it while you can, is all I can say!

Shot the net away again just after breakfast, after being fed with a couple of fresh haddocks, fried in flour, a fresh buster with golden syrup mixed with margarine running down the side of my mouth. Great memories. I returned to the fish pounds and within half an hour we had returned to the mess deck. We were sitting in the mess deck when we heard the tone of the engine change. We had become hard and fast on the seabed. Let's hope that it's not a bad fastener. The watch knocked out the warps from the block and as I strolled along the deck, I noticed that there was no weight on the after end and we have parted something but WHAT?

When the after door came up it was apparent that we had parted the bridle which connected to the dhan leno and the trawl. The fore door came up and we unclipped the quarter rope slowly. The bobbins came to the rail, slip put in and contained the net, using grummets and chains. Slowly the after end came up. Looking at the net we had got away without any net damage. We put new bridles on and shot the net away. I must say, not one word came off the bridge! I found Scotty ok and not the person people talked about. Do your job and just get on with it.

The person who had the fall is now back to 100%.

We shot and hauled the net before tea. It looked like a good catch with 50 baskets of fish.

Teatime came which I had a good tuck into as it was cowpie and mash. The meal must be my all-time favourite. You can keep your steaks, always reminds me of grandma's cooking and what better way to finish but with a nice treacle duff with runny custard. I staggering to my bunk and I gladly rolled in. I was called out at midnight.

We are now bound for home with 950 kits. This was one of the best trips that I had done in a long while!

Someone had moaned [about cleaning] at breakfast time. We are now steaming home and all the internal mats had to be put over the side, towed and then hung over the ships rails to drip dry. Being two weeks at sea, the inside used to get pongy and that is being kind. There were fish scales everywhere, so the ship needed a good clean. We operated as a team. The crew's accommodation and bridge all done during watches, with the aid coming from the 'day girls!' The decks were scrubbed with chloride lime once the nets deck boards had been stored. Brass work had been done on the bridge but lastly the ships bell had to be polished. If the Skipper inspected the ship and it was not to his standard, it all had to be done again. Finally, a bit of furniture polish was applied on the woodwork.

After the last meal had been prepared, the cook always scrubbed out the galley and silver primed the stove. Always a volunteer, I've helped out a few times, woodwork polished in the messdeck and we were already for docking.

We docked mid-afternoon, with wives and girlfriends waiting on the quayside. It was time to GO HOME. JOB DONE.

The NEXT day the fish had been landed and we made £27,000.

Who's a 'Happy Chappy'? I guess that would be me?

Random Memory

Standing in the after pounds, gutting away, when I was summoned to the bridge. Approaching the starboard wheelhouse door, I was told to take off my frock. The frock is made of oil cloth and is protective clothing used on the deck, to keeps us dry whilst working in wet conditions. I had to bend a little to pull my head through an opening, followed by my arms until it eventually slid off me. I was now wearing a light weight woolly jumper, with no sleeves, as I detested getting my arms wet whilst on the deck. Even today most of my clothing has short sleeves. I was also wearing jeans, with thigh boots.

The skipper gave me a bulb and ask me to put a new mast light in as the old bulb had blown. Apparently, this was my job, as I was the Bosun. I've never seen anywhere in writing which actually stated this but the Skipper is in charge, so I do as I'm told.

I came off the boat deck, made my way forward and continued towards the foremast towards the men in the fish pounds. I asked one of them to keep an eye on me as I stepped on the bottom rung of the mast ladders. I heard the response of 'aye-aye' followed by the sarcastic remark, that; 'you will do anything to get out of gutting the fish!'

Slowly but surely, I started to climb, soon passing the yo-yo arm which had been about the same level as the bridge. I was nearly half way up the mast. The ships heading had been head to wind and occasionally the ship would dip its head then steady itself. I hung on for dear life when this happened, then soon started to climb again, as I was on the rungs. It was like standing on your toes and I soon started to tremble. It was not the first time that I had done this but I had usually done the task whilst we had been alongside the quay.

I'm just about to climb on to the narrow part of the mast. Instead of what seemed liked ladders I have now reached simple individual steps. I had to climb up, maybe six of these, before I finally reached the mast light. There are a few different types of lights up here where I am. There was an all-round white light, then a green light for letting other ships know that we were a TRAWLER, then there was the mast light. This was the one that was faulty and I sang out to the men in the fish pounds to ask if the power had been isolated. The reply soon came back 'from he who as to be obeyed' that it was off. I slowly undid the screw which opened the light holder for me with one hand, holding on for dear life the other, twiddling with the dead light I soon changed out the bulb. The skipper shouted from the bridge window, saying that he would be switching the light back on and I'm pleased to say that the light came on.

I swiftly descended the ladders then back on terra firma. Passing the fish pounds, I noticed that a few tusks and ling, with their tongues hanging out, waiting for me now that I had finished my task. I headed up towards the bridge then slotted my frock over my head, wriggled my arms into the sleeves and this was when I had an attack of uncontrollable shaking. The skipper opened the bridge door handing me a nogging of Windjammer telling me that I had done well and thank you. My reply, 'ANYTIME!'

7

Ross Lynx

Coming out of the Ross Civet, I asked myself whether I had done the right thing. Time will soon tell. Three days at home and now I'm sailing on the Ross Lynx with Dennis Speck who always reminded me of Tommy Whitcombe in some of his ways. We had a decent crew with the general 'Rats' who I would love to name, but I'm not that type of person to 'grass' on them.

I knew a couple of the lads, for example Arty Musson, who was a great Shipmate, Kevin Hodson and a few others whose names I have forgotten for now. I'm not doing too bad, as I am remembering events which happened over 45 years ago.

On the Ross Cat. Boats I can remember the bridge set up quite clearly. Standing behind the ships wheel was steering by hand. The ships wheel had eight spokes and you had to stand behind it looking up into a binnacle compass which looked like a periscope. Just to the side of the ship's wheel we had a Mark 21 Decca Navigator which allowed us to know the position we were in. When we were at sea it worked on the principle of radio beacons all along the European coastline which transmitted signals to our apparatus. We also had a Decca plotter and every skipper had their own chart which gathered information over the years. Just behind the ship's wheel we had two times Kelvin Hughes Fish Finders which were primitive compared to more modern ships, although they were quite effective. A chart room with a radio room was directly behind the helmsman at the wheel which in turn led into the Skippers cabin. There was also a radar on the portside which gave us a coastline read-out as well as picking ships out. We had three people at any given time as watchkeepers, although this would change if we had any work to complete on the main deck. We had one toilet for the crew with only a single shower and a sit-down bath which we used mainly for washing our clothes by hand.

Usual thing of sailing mid-morning and thirty-hours later we are on the fishing grounds. We were earning a steady living with Cod, Haddock with a few mixed types of fish. We had been fishing for just over a week then we changed grounds and moved towards Foula.

Mid-morning the weather was fine with calm seas and we became fast on the seabed. The mate had rolled in and I'm in charge of the hauling of the net. The doors came up, then the dhan lenos and we pulled on the Quarter ropes, then secured the bobbins by slips and taking turns with the rope around the Cleats. It became apparent that we had something heavy in the Trawl and we soon discovered what it was.

We had caught a bag of DOGFISH that were filled with water and we had caught a great amount. We eventually used the snorkel, a named coil of ROPE. By heaving a small amount of net in we could then use another SNORKEL to repeat the process. By heaving on one and then lower the other net. On this voyage the company had taken a deckie off the ship and put a trainee in his place. As we were shorthanded the trainee had been using one of the snorkels. We heaved on the net and told the man on the snorkel to lower but on this occasion both ropes were let go together. I had my hand in the net which should have been lowered and when the rope came tight, with my hand on the knot, I tried to pull free. I eventually manage to release my hand and it came loose but not before it took off the tip [up to first joint] of my middle finger, on my right hand. My hand had been crushed in the net and all my other fingers were cut and bruised, as the net tightened.

Fortunately, I had no broken bones, or even worse still I could have been pulled over the side. The quick thinking of one of the lads, who put turns on the winch to stop the net from pulling me and maybe others, over the side. I was guided off the deck and I was not in any pain, just the skin had been removed, leaving a bone protruding from my hand. The glove had gone and was never seen again. The Mate was called and he looked at my hand and said I needed medical attention and would have to be taken off the ship.

I was sitting in the messdeck with a sweet cup of tea, a smoke and was pain free, as I've already stated. I decided I needed to clean-up and have a change of gear. I must thank Arty Musson who was a God send as he helped me to get cleaned-up and to pack my gear.

From Foula I was put onto a small pilot boat. I had to climb up a quay wall and then onto a tractors trailer. I was driven about 20 miles to Lerwick Hospital to receive medical attention. I stayed overnight at the Seamans Mission and the next day was on a flight to Aberdeen. From the airport I had to take a taxi to an Agent's Office in Aberdeen who provided me with a train warrant to go home.

I then spoke to the wife to let her know that I was ok and not to worry. I gave her details of train times and my ETA but this would mean that I would arrive at Doncaster station at midnight. There were no connections to Grimsby until 0630 hours. Unbeknown to me the wife arranged for me to be picked up by car and I arrived home early morning.

When I finally arrive home it was then that the shock hit me. I was shacking uncontrollably and was feeling very sick. I had the first digit of my middle finger amputated with only local anaesthesia and had stitches in every finger of my right hand which was bruised and swollen. Both of my knees were badly bruised where I had pushed against the ships side to get my hand free of the net. If I had not used all my strength, I believe that I would have gone over the side. If I had not been collected from Doncaster by a member of the family, I really don't know what state I would have been in.

The next day my mother-in-law gave the ships runner Hell because they had made me make that journey whilst injured.

I was told by the crew to look after myself and get well and not to worry as they wouldn't be claiming shorthand money, as I would not be there. Guess what, twenty hours after the ship docked things seemed to change. At the time of my accident and when I left the ship, we had 1,000 kits of fish on board. When I went to pick up my share, I only received a quarter of my money.

I must admit that NEVER in my career fishing have I ask for SHORTHAND money, when through no fault of their own, a person had to be put ashore.

After injuring my hand which took nearly seven months to heal, with numerous operations (well 2) it was now finally healing. I can't praise Dr Renfrew enough as he provided new dressing every three days which had been changed/supplied by my GP. I had been summoned by the Health Board who sent me for an interview and tests. After an examination of nearly an hour I was told that I was fit for work. The Doctor who examined me did not examine or even look at my injured hand and merely looked at my general fitness. I went on the dock and gave the result to Dr Renfrew and he gave them hell, saying that I needed to have 100 per cent use of my hand and that HE would say when I would be fit to return to sea.

All the time I had been ashore money was scarce. Cheryl and I tried to get additional help [believe it was called Income Support]. We had an interview which lasted about three hours in the Social where they wanted to know 'basically what we had for breakfast' and to look at our bank accounts, household expenses, utility bills etc. This was not a problem as we didn't have much left as I had been injured for so long. After the interview I was advised that we were entitled to help. I had been awarded 20 pence per week extra. In the cubicle next to me, a mother had been there asking for help for daughter who had been in prison (thieving) and she was soon to be released. She had been given a flat, monies to buy furniture and food with cash to help her. There I was, in Dire Straits, no Income Support, just sick pay, I was not very happy.

Dr Renfrew decided that I was fit to return to work.

I never spoke to any of that crew again and if they saw me, they would cross over to the other side of the road.

Not all fishermen are like this, may I add, usually FRIENDS FOR LIFE but not on this OCCASION!

Comment added on by Cheryl Telford:

What you haven't said in your 'tales of old' is that, following the amputation of the first digit of your middle finger and the bodged job that Lerwick Hospital did stitching up the wound, you were off work for seven months. When you had the wound dressed for the first time at Grimsby Hospital, they were shocked by what they saw. In their opinion, they said, the wound should have been operated on under general anaesthetic and should have had more bone removed to make a flap over the end of the finger.

As we all know - no work - no pay and nothing from the 'Company'.

After several months you were summoned for an interview with the Social Security Doctor's to establish whether you were fit for work. I recall that you came back from the interview and said that the Doctor had examined you thoroughly but had not once looked at your hand. When you pointed out that you were 'off sick' because of the injury to your hand he said he just had to tick the boxes on the form. It seemed that your hand was not on the form. From the examination they decided that you were fit for work and stopped your sick pay.

I clearly remember Dr Renfrew getting on the phone and raising 'Merry Hell' with Social Security for stopping your Sick pay. In no uncertain terms he told them that HE and ONLY HE would decide when you were fit to return to work and if you went back to sea with your hand as it was, you would probably lose your arm and even your life. They reinstated your sick pay and you had to have two further operations on your hand. The Good Old Days - or so they say!!! Thank goodness we had a good family to support us during this difficult time.

Random Memory

I recollect that prior to being in The Ross Lynx I had been in the GRIMSBY LADY. It seemed an age ago that I had been in the 'Lady' and I had not been out 'suited and booted' since leaving this very special ship.

After being declared 'fit for work' and 'signing on' I decided we should go out and get dressed up. I put on my best suit and waistcoat and as I put my hand in one of the pockets of the waistcoat, I found nearly £50.

On our last trip, in the Lady, we received our settlings partly by cheque and partly in cash and some of the bills had been £50 notes. I recall getting a round in and I paid with a £50 note (I wanted to change it to smaller notes) and I must have put the change in my waistcoat pocket. We had a really good night and I remember saying to Cheryl that I had spent quite a lot of money! I did not think any more about it.

The wife would always check my pockets before taking my suits to the dry cleaners and when I found the money, she said she had not taken the waistcoat to the cleaners as I didn't wear it very often. She did say that she wished she had because we could have really used that money whilst I was injured. We had struggled so much during this time and we had all that money sitting in my pocket! We laughed about it and now the wife ALWAYS checks my pockets but never finds any treasure.

Just shows when hardship comes you pull together as a family. We had no luxuries but things are now on the up. That's why I love this woman so much, she is so strong and we both pull together as a team.

8

Ross Panther

0100 hours knock on the door and it's effing Sizer. Shall I tell him to eff off? I don't know why but I never liked that man. I remember settling up one day and Sizer asked if I needed dropping off as he was going to the rank to look for fares. I jumped in and he dropped me at Riby Square Rank. As I was leaving, he tried to get me to pay him. I told him to 'Fuck Off' this time.

When I was taken down dock to sail, I approached Charlie Ward, a ships Runner and told him not to send him to pick me up anymore.

I climbed over the whaleback ladders, kitbag over my shoulder, found my berth quickly and put my gear away. Then onto the quay to Coleridge's for a few bits and pieces. We were now given gear issues for wet gear and bedding. This was only issued with 'number of days at sea'. I got my usual things, tin baccy, Sven Hassle novel, not forgetting Edge, a new breed of cowboy, then back onboard for a quick coffee. I looked into the aft focsal and introduced myself. I knew most of the crew. The mate shouted out from the alleyway that we were sailing. I went onto the bridge and said morning to the Skipper and was greeted with a grunt. I felt sure that he had had a good drink but I soon found out that he had not and the reason being that this was his 'normal'.

Just clear of the lightship when the Skipper (not to be named) took the wheel off me saying; 'Go tell the mate to come up with his watchmates. He can have the first watch!' Off the bridge, down the ladders, through the engine room, looked in the galley and saw Dixie Loveridge, the cook, making bread. We were an hour out of the dock! He just said 'Standards!'

Now down the accommodation ladders. The mate's not in his cabin but with the crew in the after focsal, just necking a dram. He asked, 'How are you getting on with the Skipper?' I told him that I thought he seemed kind of weird! He said 'You'll soon get used to him!' I gave him the message and off he went with his two watchmates, who I didn't know but had seen knocking around the local pubs etc. I was offered a can of beer by Scarborough John which I declined saying that I wanted a cuppa instead. He had been sitting with a cockney sounding lad, I think they called him Steve and another chirpy lad, who came from down south, I think it could be Brighton. He went by the name of Ducko always up for a laugh. I've known him from the mid-70s to present day. He is married to Sandra, a lovely lady, who supports his football team 'the Seagulls' but hates mollies!

I bid my farewells and went back to the mess and had a cuppa. I looked in the after berth and there was another four-man cabin on the port quarter. I said my hellos and knew some faces but not names again but it was a youngish crew. I think that this will be a happy crew to sail with. Time will tell. I went below and was sharing a cabin with the cook who let me have the bottom bunk. Rolled in, looking forward to a few hours kip which soon passed when I was called out at teatime for my watch.

As we took over the watch, the Skipper came out of his cabin with a slam of the bridge door, as he went down the bridge ladders and the same in the Engine room. SLAM! I was wandering; 'Is it me!' But Scarborough John said; 'No it's not you he's always like this. You've heard Fuck all, wait till we get fishing!' SLAM! Engine room door, up came the Skipper with a quick 'Grunt'. I was told to look at the Skipper's night orders. SLAM! Went the Skipper's cabin door. Are we sailing with Larry Grayson; 'SHUT THAT DOOR!'

My watch went by without any slamming of doors and lockers. Listening to radio Luxembourg with all the up-and-coming artists. This time tomorrow we should be fishing. Let's hope that we can earn a living and most of all get home safely. We seem to have a happy crew with the exception of the NUTTER on the BRIDGE!

Breakfast had just been eaten and after we had finished, the call came to shoot the nets. The trawl doors were put out, quickly followed by the net and weights. Soon we were paying the warps away with a shout from the bridge 250 fathoms of warp which was needed to reach the sea bed. The last 50 had been shouted and the ship eased in. We attached the messenger hook onto the forward warp which in turn would pick up the after warp, taking it into the towing block. Soon after the cry came from aft that we were 'All Square aft!'.

Let's hope that we can get a good trip in and I can come off the ship. We seem to have a good crew but the atmosphere from the bridge is not very good at this moment in time. The Bond had been dished out, 6 cans of beer including smokes, fag papers, a few bits of confectionery, just a basic issue if truth be told. Just had time to put my bond away and we came fast.

After coming hard and fast, shouting and kicking off with what sounded like the ship's bulwarks being banged and kicked. This could be heard by all of us on the working deck. The Skipper was having another paddy or so it seemed. We soon came clear of the obstacle on the seabed. With thick mud on the trawl doors, it seems that we had dug into a mudbank. The trawl was pulled up to the cod ends then lowered back into the water. With the gear back in the water we all went aft where the Mate had been waiting for me, he told me; 'Don't take it personally. If you hear unusual noises etc. it's not aimed at any one person.' Over the next few days things seemed to settle down and we are earning a steady living with just the odd mutter from the command post. The Mate seemed to have a calming influence on the Skipper as he had sailed with him over the years.

After nearly a week away we have a problem down the engine room and are having to run into Scalloway for repairs. Walter, the ships agent met us in and we were told to get a basket of fish for him which soon appeared on the quayside. The Skipper and Mate went ashore mainly to have a phone call home. I was left in charge with the order not to let anyone ashore. Whilst we were alongside a lorry pulled up and the lads were talking to the driver. The next thing fish was been put into the lorry with money being exchanged on the quayside. The Skipper and Mate returned saying the part for the engine won't be here until breakfast and that the lads could go ashore.

After our tea some went for a shower, others didn't bother and by 2000 hours we were walking up the hill towards the Scalloway Hotel and Pub. We had some strange looks from the locals but as soon as they knew we were off the ship in the Harbour, they accepted us. The money from the fish sales came in handy with only a few of us who knew the score we set out to enjoy ourselves.

Soon it was closing time and we had to return back to the ship. Halfway down the road, in a field, stood a Shetland pony. We ventured towards it. Someone dared me to ride it and not being one to refuse a dare I sat on it. Immediately it rear-ended its back legs, throwing me off. Laughter was had by all, except me, who had lost my pride but I soon saw the funny side. The pony was unharmed and coming away from the field a car pulled up behind us and followed us back to the ship. As we climbed back onboard the Police rolled down a window laughing at us, saying; 'It looks like you have had a good night!' The next morning, we sailed before lunch, waking up without any hangover but feeling rough.

After ten hard working days, the voice from the bridge shouted 'Drop the doors in. Lash her up. We're going HOME!'. We had 850 kits down the fish room, most of the Cat Boats have averaged the same as us. The deck was cleared with most of the deck boards put away. Bridge watches were set with my watch finished at 1830 hours. I had my tea with the rest of the crew, I had a few hours off till my next watch at 0300am. During the afternoon watch the Skipper pulled me aside in to his cabin telling me to close the door. I was then asked if I wanted a regular job and I replied that I would let you know before we dock.

After thirty hours I was called to the bridge to steer the ship in the river and up to the landing Berth. I then gave the skipper my answer regarding a regular berth, which had to be NO. I told him that I wouldn't sail across the dock with him, as I had been on edge all trip, with HIS TANTRUMS but I would miss the crew. They were a great bunch of lads. On landing day, I went down dock and made a decent trip.

I was asked by Bill Battie if I would be going back. My stern reply was 'Not a chance. The Skipper is effing mental!'

He replied; 'Ross Leopard. Next Wednesday. Skipper Jimmy Brown.'

THAT WILL DO NICELY!

9

Ross Leopard

Went down dock yesterday to sign on where I met Jim Brown, the Skipper. He asked me which ship I had come out of and I told him Ross Panther. He was saying that a few skippers have had run-ins with him but he had increasingly got worse now that a few Deep-Water Skippers were coming into these ships. It had been at a time when some Skippers had retired. J. P. had passed away, Alan Redpath was semi-retired and so was Dennis Loveday, just to name a few.

As I was leaving, I was asked if I wanted a lift up dock. The car was either a Ford Cortina or Galaxy. I was dropped off at the Humber Hotel and he came in for a pint with me. We spoke over the drink, saying that he had a decent crew and that I would fit in nicely. He then dropped me off at the Clee Park. I was feeling pleased with myself, although it was only going to be for two trips relieving which later made the way for me to go in the Jackal, (which I will write about later).

Taxi came at 0300 hours. Opened the door there stood Snowy Parker and he told me that we would not be sailing due to an engine room problem. He advised me to either telephone the office in the morning or pop down and they will tell us what's happening. I was pleased as I didn't feel like sailing anyway! I went back inside, just making a cuppa when the wife came down stairs and I gave her the good news. It looks like we will have the WEEKEND AT HOME!

At last, we have sailed. The ships runner, Charlie Ward, picked me up at 0600 hours. The usual routine of saying my goodbyes, kissing both the kids and telling them that I loved them dearly. They don't seem to understand, as yet, why I have to go away to sea to earn monies for a better lifestyle. This only happened if we have a good catch and hit a favourable market.

I don't seem to use the outfitters on the North Wall, as I am getting the things, I need from Tiplady's or Gerald Baileys. As I have had issues with those on the North Wall.

Only been aboard a little while when I was summoned to the Bridge. I took my place behind the ships wheel following orders on the Helm. The lads on deck were putting the yo-yo up (out hauler to pull the net into the sea) as we entered the river Humber. With plenty of shipping, we gradually made our way to the lightship.

The Mate, Derek Hack took over and relieved me, saying that my next watch would be at tea time. I slowly made my way aft seeing a few familiar faces. The cook was preparing a pan of shackles for dinner and I grabbed a quick cuppa with a cheese sarnie. The shore bread was tasteless and it was like eating putty. The cheap shite sold at Netto. George Herd were the Ship Chandlers, I seem to remember. He had his hands into most fishing companies. I ended up eating the cheese without the bread. I can't remember the cook's name. We shared the same cabin and I had the lower bunk, so no climbing for me.

Although I had a decent sleep, I always felt tired after we had sailed. Sleep soon came. Just after midday I went into the messdeck and met a few of the crew whilst enjoying the stew. I knew a couple of lads from previous trips and some who I had not sailed with before. I then went and rolled in again reading the latest novel by Sven Hassle. In the after cabin the lads were having a can or two, then the portable record player came out playing all this trips hits.

Uneventful evening watch. I had a big pan of shackles for my tea. Little Brendan was on watch with me. I'm sure that he was from Southern Ireland. I told him to talk slowly and I would then be able to understand what he was saying. There were plenty of lights in the distance coming from the oil and gas rigs. Lots of Skippers were complaining as they are putting platforms up on the fishing grounds which have been used for generations by fishermen.

A quick handover at 2300 hours and then my watch retreated from the bridge to go aft to the accommodation. I rolled in before midnight and there was no noise coming from the after focsal. I soon fell asleep and woke up mid-morning. I had a quick smoke and a cuppa then slowly made my way on deck. The Skipper spotted me and called me on to the bridge where he told me to condemn the cod ends and to make a new set. The weather was fine so I went back on to the deck and stripped the cod ends. The lads went off deck for a quick brew and on return came to give me a hand, saying, tongue in cheek; 'You will have to give us a can for helping!' My reply was; 'But of course.'

Just before lunch the bond was issued. I was issued a case of beer and a large nogging of rum which went down nicely. I had a can of beer whist putting my bond away. The daymen caught me and I handed three cans to them. In return they said that I was the best bosun sailing from Grimsby. I replied; 'You're only having the one can.' Lunch was shouted and I was sitting in the mess. The Skipper came in saying that he would take my watch whilst I carried on with the cod ends. He kept Paddy on the bridge whilst my other watchmate came on the deck with me. Quickly the cod ends came together, chafers on, new cowhides, halving becket with chains. I was told to rig the halving becket 26 meshes and up which in contrast being about 60 baskets of fish. Finally, cod end meshes were put on mid-afternoon and all completed. The Skipper shouted out: 'That was smart!' It would have taken a lot longer if I had not dished out a can of beer to the three daymen. Cod line tied, net secured and we should be fishing just before breakfast.

Bloody cable-laid warps. The Skipper came and looked at the towing block seeing how the trawl cables were laying. We both agreed that the fore door had travelled over the after door causing the trouble.

The Skipper told us to standby, knocking the wires out of the towing block. First, we gathered speed, went hard to port, trying to take the turns out. We could see three at first. Then the ship straightened up, eased down the speed and we had taken two turns out. The order then came to knock out and heave on the warps. Soon the warp, with the doors appearcd, showing that the warp had been hanging over the trawl door. We unshipped the winch, let the warps go quickly into the sea, meanwhile pulling the slack warp off, shipped the warps up again. heaving away and it soon became apparent that we had cleared the doors. We brought the rest of the net up and with a quick visual inspection the net was back on the sea bed. With 'ALL SQUARE' being shouted from the TOWING BLOCK.

JUST one of the daily HAZARDS that can happen.

NOTE: Just to stop any confusion:

When the trawl doors are lowered into the water, they keep the spread of the trawl mouth open, where hopefully the fish will end up.

Having cable laid warps is when lowering the trawl doors down, sometimes the paravane and instead of keeping the net open the trawl mouth closes up.

I hope it helps those that haven't been to SEA.

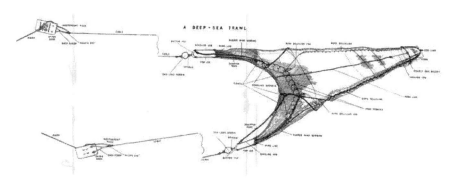

A Deep Sea Trawl

I have just eaten a large bowl of Halibut soup, dipping fresh busters, lathered in margarine (only allowed butter on a Sunday).

We started hauling the net at 1300 hours. I knocked the warps out of the towing block whilst my two watchmates guided the warp onto the winch barrel. The Mate is on the deck standing by the winch. Last fifty fathoms of warp were called by the Mate and the Skipper said he would spin round on the bridles which only took a few minutes. The sea had been more or less calm with a light breeze just glaring over the ships rail when the sea began to show signs of white bubbles which indicates that we have caught a large haul of fish.

The Mate at the winch began heaving the warps in slowly until the trawl doors were hanging on their safety chains. Soon the dhan lenos came up, then the bobbins laid on the deck with both myself and the mate using the snorkeler rope until the fish in the trawl had been contained in the trawl's belly with a bowling knot tied around the belly. The Skipper gave a kick astern whilst we grabbed the halving becket extension line. The first bag of fish came aboard, followed swiftly by five more which in total was about 300 baskets of extra-large coley. The sweat was running out of me (I believe it would have been late February time). Soon other ships came in the area where we were fishing. Some were catching as much as us and some not so lucky. The fish, giant coley or saithe, were nearly all five to six feet long. Good fish to put down the fish room.

We put the trawl back over the side once more and started to clean the fish. Some of the crew couldn't throw them into the washer, landing just over the deck boards. After about two and a half hours of gutting the fish, we had cleared as much as 200 baskets of fish. We hauled mid-afternoon with about another 50 baskets. Teatime soon came. I went on the bridge to relieve the skipper for his tea. He returned and said we would be hauling again after tea. We caught 200 baskets in that haul. I quickly had my tea and promptly rolled in. I was called out at midnight with 200 baskets on the deck. Thinking to myself; 'We will soon fill her up' which is just what we did but we didn't land at Grimsby!

The Otter Door

1,000 baskets in a little over twenty-four hours. Thank heavens for such large coley. Not just me but a couple of the lads have been down the fish room to give them a drag out. The fish room man has only been up for his meals, staying down during hauling time, getting ice and boards ready. We all have arms like Arnie but the elder crew are just putting the fish over the boards not even attempting to throw any into the washer. When we have finished cleaning the fish, the fish in the middle, are thrown down the hatch by the rest of the crew. Last haul we had a large hole in the belly head. It must have been caused by a boulder with the net being so chaffed. Whilst we were mending, all the fish in the middle were cleared and we now have only 50 baskets of fish on deck. Maybe we will get a breather after we have shot the net away and hopefully clear the pounds.

Cod ends are back over the side and most of us are working like Zombies. Everything is aching, especially our backs and shoulders. We have had plenty of fish scales in our eyes and sticking on to our arms etc. During mealtimes one or two of the lads have bobbed off eating their meals. Coming off a cold deck into the warmth, exhaustion suddenly overwhelms you.

On the deck you are sometimes like robots, picking up the fish by its gills, cutting the neck and running your knife down the fish. On opening, taking out the intestines, lifting the livers out, putting them into a basket, also making sure to have taken the heart and clots, double nape and throwing into the washer. When the ship rolls to starboard, the fish is thrown into the washer which assists in a distance thrown. I have just had my tea and now it's time to roll in. Boots off, jumper off and straight into my bunk. I can't be bothered with any reading. I have a quick smoke, turn my bunk light out and hopefully dream of better things.

I was called out at midnight with 40 baskets of coley. We have been on the fish for a couple of days, with every joint in my body aching. What I wouldn't give for a long soak in a radox bath. Just putting my thigh boots on and I have cramp in both legs. I am now walking like John Wayne, without a gun or a horse! I had a quick roll up and a cuppa and ventured on to the foredeck. The first thing I noticed was that the washer was turned around with the fish now going down the forward fish room. The weather has been excellent and we have even seen the Northern lights, giving us a short display. Always marvelled as various colours drifted across the sky.

The Mate came out of the fish room. He had just been called on to the Bridge to relieve the Skipper and he told me how much warp had been paid out last haul and to pop on the bridge for the evening issue of Rum. Just after 0130 hours my watch had our dram of rum and we won't be hauling till 0300 hours so it was time to rest our aching bodies. Nobody was catching great amounts or so it seemed. Hauling time was soon upon us. I slowly made my way to the winch tools to hold the last 25 fathom of warp (short mark). I was soon told to commence heaving. The doors came up, the rest of the net surfaced with 50 or 60 baskets of coley with a sprinkling of white fish being cod and haddock. We had soon shot the net away again. One of the crew cleaned the messdeck and the galley to enable the cook to have a clean start for the following day! We don't want to upset the COOK. Soon the smell of fresh bread came to us in the fish pounds.

After an hour's gash sleep on the seat locker and feeling ache free, as such, I heard a commotion coming from the messdeck. A certain person, who shall remain nameless (other than Brendon) had started to have a go at a couple of senior deckies. Without messing about I pulled him out of the situation and backhanded him (no witnesses). Every ship he goes in, he causes aggro. I've had a few dealings with him before. He, thinks he's a mighty midget but this time he came unstuck. People who know me, know I'm not a violent person but, let's put it this way, I've always been able to look after myself.

Soon we were hauling in the nets. Nearly mid-morning with another big haul of 180 baskets or so of the same fish. Big coley, full of roe and chicklings. All the species coming from the deep-water to spawn in shallower waters. Soon we were all square with the gear back in the water. Called onto the Bridge for the rum issue. The Skipper asked; 'Have you had a problem with someone?' I said; 'Who me?' (With a SMILE on my face).

All settled in the fish pounds, when we heard a mighty shout. One of the senior deckies, was chucking a fish into the washer when it allegedly 'slipped out of his grip' hitting Brendan on the back of his head. Nobody laughed!

The Fish Room

Just before lunch we had nearly cleared all the fish away. All hands, barring the watch, went for lunch which was the main meal and was cowpie with all the trimmings. I covered mine with brown sauce to give it an extra kick.

I wish that I hadn't eaten it because when we hauled the cod ends, they were up with the trawl doors. Six bags of fish had been the outcome. The net went back over. We all went back into the fish. About mid-afternoon we hauled again with another 150 baskets of fish. The Skipper sent an extra dram round to lift the morale of the crew. Teatime soon came upon us and I relieved the Skipper for his tea and then had mine. I was called out at midnight and we are bound to land the fish, of all places, in Bremerhaven as there is too much coley being landed in the UK.

Breakfast time and all the fish had been put away down the fish room. The Mate reckons we have 1,650 to 1,700 kits of fish, as we only have one bay left in the fish room. I'm glad the weather's a fine westerly, 3 to 4. I'm sure that the propellor is nearly out of the water as there is a lot of shuddering from the aft side. After breakfast we went back on the deck and gave the decks a good wash down, as we had cleared all the deck boards, gratings and the washer have been put away. The yo-yo has been topped and we are more or less ready for docking. Seems strange going across to Germany, when usually we hug the east side coastline.

We have all noticed how cold it is getting. Rumours are that the German fish dock area had frozen waters. It's certainly feeling cold enough.

Since early morning we have been in a dense fog. The pilot launch is just coming alongside us. What a size, it is nearly as big as ourselves. We have three miles to run and I've been ordered to take the steering. As we started to approach the land, we notice that the sea around the harbour looked frozen over and we soon discovered that it was. A small icebreaker ahead of us broke the ice to help us to enter and get penned into the lock gates. Twenty minutes later we were taken to our landing berth. Customs Officers came aboard, paperwork was inspected and away they went. Next came the foreman lumper with his team who were soon going about their trade and getting the landing gear ready.

On the quayside were a couple of grocery men wanting our custom and both held trays with different pastries and bread buns, as tasters. Both came aboard speaking to the cook. The agent came aboard and spoke with an accent similar to American. I left the bridge and went straight into the mess deck and proceeded filling my face with what looked and tasted like Danish pastries. I soon grabbed a couple of hours sleep whilst I had the chance. I rolled out just before tea, had a quick shower and a change of clothes. I washed a few bits in the sit-down bath, rinsed them and hung them over a make shift washing line. A few of the lads have gone ashore to look for the local ale houses.

Just after 2200 hours the first of the fish came out of the hold, all looking in pristine condition. I went ashore with the Mate looking at the fish being weighed and sorted. From the corner of my eye, I saw a movement of someone trying to attract our attention. I strolled over to where the person had been. He was in a Volkswagen and when he opened the sides, we discovered that it had been turned into a portable bar with racks of snaps of various flavours together with a few bears. I sampled a few and said our goodbyes. I rolled in for the night, waking around breakfast time, feeling refreshed.

Just after 0200 hours all the fish has been taken out of the fish room. I couldn't get much sleep as it was so cold with just the harbour generator being on and the continuous noise as the fish holds were being emptied. We were a bit short of the tally with 1,620 kits or about 90 tons or there about.

After breakfast I had a quick stroll ashore with a few Deutschmarks in my pocket. I noticed how clean and spotless everything was coming from the dock area to the town centre which only took a few moments. I found a small shop which was selling porcelain dolls and I went inside and purchased one for my daughter and found a present for my son and wife. I had to be back on board before lunch as we are sailing at 1300 hours. Lunchtime soon approached and one or two of the lads were walking around like zombies after tasting the local ales. Most of them had been drinking Dortmund Eff and others.

Little did we know that by this time tomorrow we would have both sides of the deck full again with coley! We finally sailed at 1350 hours, clear of the lock gates and away to sea. There was just a small amount of ice about but as we leave the land the weather begins to clear with the visibility over 15 miles. We are now in the traffic separation zones. Tea time now approaching.

The main decks with the boards, washer, with the fish room, now already for part two of this trip. We were told that we had made £24,000 but our office say we made £22,000! Robbing gits but who are we to argue with them. Little Paddy has started again and I noticed that he has a lovely black eye but it's not from me THIS TIME wink, wink!

0600 hours called out to shoot the trawl again. Less than 20 hours we are back at FOULA which is a fishing area just West of the Shetland Islands. The trawl has now been put over the side, the doors lowered, 'All square!' shouted from the after end. I was standing alongside the trawl brakes whilst they cooled down and within ten minutes sitting having our breakfast which was eggs, gammon, German sausages, with fresh bread rolls. The Mate came off the bridge telling us that the ships are not catching so much. Just as he had finished speaking the warps were screaming out, we have come FAST!

Coming fast usually means that we have either dug the doors into the seabed or come stuck on an obstruction on the seabed or having picked up some boulders etc. The order was given to knock out the warps in the block. I took this opportunity of having a couple of smokes with a cuppa which I took to the winch with me whilst I had the chance, as one never knows when the occasion will present itself.

Slowly but surely, we heaved on the winch. Suddenly we became clear of the problem. The trawl doors came up and with a whooshing sound the cod ends appeared, like a whale jumping out of the water. Slowly it began to settle on the surface and plenty of coley had come free of the net just lying on the surface. Bobbins came in with a large hole in the belly head. We must have caught a shoal of fish and with a bit of a struggle we managed to get a rope around the rest of the belly and baiting's. Soon taking the first bag of fish out, then putting a lashing around the top part of the cod ends so as not to let the cod ends go back over. We did this seven times.

The fish pounds were all full on the starboard side and we had to stop the job by putting gratings with boards in the port foredeck. Now after moving the boards from the starboard foredeck, the fish began going to the portside area. Two more bags of fish were taken on board. I am now sunk into the fish with my feet touching the deck. I'm well and truly stuck but by holding onto the cod ends I was slowly pulled out. Tying the cod line, the Skipper shouted down to lace the broken net together.

To be honest I'm just about knackered with sweat pouring from me. This time yesterday we had been sailing from Bremerhaven, now we are up to our thighs again with the same type of fish we have just landed. We have around 400 baskets on board, with the net only being in the water for no longer than 20 minutes total. The Skipper sang out that we were laying for an hour or so, enabling us to clear a few baskets away. I went aft to get my gutting knife, with a quick smoke and on returning to the deck the rum bottle appeared with the Skipper saying, 'Just for the DECK CREW and the COOK!'

We have now been fishing for just two and a half days and we have just turned the fish washer around. Now filling the forward part of the fish room. I can't say which part of my body aches more. My shoulders and arms feeling heavy, legs cramping up due to standing upright in the fish pounds for long hours. Making things a little harder when gutting coley. It's like cutting through leather and we are needing to keep our knives sharp at all times. We are not catching big bags of fish but averaging 50/60 baskets for 3-hour tows.

The first twenty-four hours had been very hectic with nearly a thousand baskets of fish on board. We are all very tired but spirits are high. Of course, we moan and complain but we just get on with the job in hand, especially as the rum has taken off (run out) and we are now having German Brandy. It's an acquired taste but I'm not enjoying it as much.

I am loving the German food which is all top quality unlike George Herds offerings. I've learnt my lesson by not eating so much during the day but I make up for it at teatime, as this is my watch below. It's getting to the stage where I have my tea, get called out at midnight, then most of the time I don't get to bed until teatime the next day. I can't really complain. It's the life that we have all chosen.

Just had my watch off and called out with the weather being kind. Glimmer of the Northern Lights trying to make an appearance. The Mates on the bridge whilst the Skipper goes below. Everything is good. The trawl net came up with about 40 baskets of fish, mostly coley, with a few cod and haddocks mixed in. All square by 0100 hours then into the fish pounds. Nice steady living, with the next haul about the same.

Breakfast soon came upon us and mid-morning we hauled and up with the doors came 250 baskets. The Skipper shouted out just after lunch that we will be landing in Bremerhaven on Friday, giving us just twenty-four hours more work before we leave. Effing knackered and looking forward to some home time. Docked in Bremerhaven at 1600 hours, turning out 1,550 kits of mostly coley. Just after the fish had been landed, we sailed to Grimsby.

0600 hours we left the coastline, hoping to dock in Grimsby just before the midnight tide. During the day the ship had been cleaned inside and out. Just after midnight we docked, tying up under one of the ice chutes as we are now completely empty. Good news for the fish room, staff having all fresh ice for next trip.

From the bridge I saw the wife on the quay. I climbed off the ship with all my washing, smokes etc. As I went up to the wife, I put a bottle of brandy into her handbag and in an instant a Custom Officer appeared saying that I had put something in her bag. I said that it was a bottle of beer. He asked the wife if that was right and she nodded her head, meaning that she agreed with me. He then wanted to see in my kit bag and I showed him I had a doll for my daughter and a gift for my wife and son and some smokes. He said OK and then waved us away. When we got in the car the wife said: 'Don't ever do that again!' I said that I wouldn't, and I showed her that I had another bottle of brandy in my bag. She was not amused.

We had a goodnights sleep. The wife went to work just after 00800 hours and I took the children to school. Just after 1100 hours I walked into the Clee Park front room and the usual figures were there. Around one table sat Sid Brennan, a few of his brothers with a couple of the Carter family.

Mid-day I walked down dock to settle up. We had made just over £44,000 for just over 18 days dock to dock. We are having four days in dock sailing mid-morning. I picked up my settlings putting most of it in the Bank. Gone are the days of my youth, when having plenty of money meant I had of hangers on who all expect a treat. I now have responsibilities, having a wife, two children and a mortgage.

I met the wife at lunchtime in the White Knight and when she went back to work, I went to the White Bear. The Skipper and his wife were there with a few of the crew. I had a couple of drinks then decided to go home as I promised the wife that we would be going to Steeles Restaurant for a landing day treat for the kids.

Later on in the day I heard that our Skipper had gone to his Bank to get some monies for his holiday and that he had been mugged just outside the pub. Somebody must have been watching his every move. Just shows that you have to be careful. That's why I only used pubs where people knew me and would keep an eye on me!

How nice and peaceful watching the kids with a bit of home time away from the harsh conditions which as a trawlerman we encountered. I am quite content to sit at home with the family. I no longer have to be in the pub from opening to closing time, pissing all my hard-earned money down the drain, as I have a homelife and family.

Better get my gear sorted as I have just had that dreaded telephone call saying crew are to be picked up at 0900 hours. Derek Hack is taking her away this trip. Mind you, he had been Mate last trip. Looking forward to sailing. Most Fishermen got fed up at home, not with homelife but with having nothing to do. When we were at home, we wished that we were at sea and when we were at sea, we would wish we were at home. Catch 22 comes to mind. Roll on Friday of this week.

It is my last night in dock and just checking that I have all my gear in my kit bag. I don't use the one that we used to throw over our shoulders and I now have a medium canvas zip type which makes things easier, as I can see what's inside. I've said my goodbyes to all the family and relatives which I think is very important as it could be the last time that they see me. Strange things happen at sea, as we all have known, especially with the conditions in which we have to work. Such is the price of fish.

I never really had a good sleep the night before sailing, especially when it is an early morning pick up. I seemed to be half awake and not quite asleep just in case I missed the taxi driver. However, on this occasion I woke up naturally, just after breakfast. Same old, same old, had a dozen fags and numerous cups of coffee. When the time we were ordered came, I would start marching up and down the dining room, looking out of the window, awaiting the dreaded taxi. It finally arrived twenty minutes late with Sizer being the driver. I opened the door and told him that I'm not getting in the car with him and basically told him to fluff off. He told me that I would still be getting charged for the pick-up but in the end I didn't. After he left Charlie Ward [Ships Runner] came and took me down dock. He apologised for sending Sizer to my house as he knew I did not like him.

I finally arrived on the quayside, went up the dreaded ladder and within twenty minutes we were heading out the dock. I'm not sure but I think that Terry Horrocks had been the new Mate but I can't be certain.

Whilst steaming to the lightship the washer and yoyo were put up, scupper doors were lifted as we are heading into a northerly gale. I was relieved on the bridge at lunch time and we were just passing Hornsea and Withernsea. A full English breakfast had been put out for lunch which went down a treat. I finished putting my work gear away. I can't really get used to sharing a cabin with the cook, maybe it's because I've been spoilt having my own cabin. Now time to grab an hour as I will be going on watch at teatime as the watches have been split, each watch doing three hours each. Tea time back to normal. Had a quick smoke, quick glance through a small war comic, I don't think that I read much. Falling asleep then being woken up to the shout of 'TEA O!'

I went on watch at 1830 hours. The weather is now a northerly force 6 and smack on the nose a loud noise is coming from the Whaleback. The bloody anchor has come loose. I was sent forward, with both my watch mates, whilst the skipper took the watch. The ship is now running down the wind at a slow speed. We climbed up onto the whaleback and noticed straightaway that the anchor had come loose and that there was no cement around the spurling pipe. We started the windlass and took up the slack chain. A few rags were put into the spurling pipe which was then topped with cement. We decided to put a piece of tarpaulin around the cement and to make sure that the area was clear. We then proceeded aft and eventually back on to the bridge. With a thankyou I took over the Watch and we are now heading back on our original course N 1/2 W.

After putting our position down, using the Decca Navigator, I took over the wheel. All these types of ships had been 'Hand Steering' but I seem to remember that they had trials with an automatic system on the Zebra. We are now all settled down again. We have just passed Whitby and Scarborough and now we are starting to lose sight of the coastline. A few fishing boats are running into the land.

One of my watch-mates was sent to make a pot of tea with the tea that we purchase from the bond. I had some left over from mu last voyage and it tastes a lot better than the tea we are given which consisted of large leaves with sticks. The tea was put in to an empty milk can and topped up with sugar. Once made, half a tin of evaporated milk was added and some may find it disgusting but at least it kept us warm.

The weather is really beginning to freshen up and must be a 7 or 8 now with water being tossed onto the whaleback. I hope that the cement has set. At 2300 hours I put the position on the chart. The Mate came to relieve me and I signed off on the radio log. I then made my way aft along with my crew mates. I don't think that we are going to get much sleep by the way that the ship is dipping and diving.

Bloody hell - what a NIGHT! Hardly anyone has had any sleep, so I wasn't by myself. The wind is now North Westerly 8/9 and we are being thrown about like peas in a pisspot. The noise of pots and pans could be heard coming from the galley. The cook has been out twice to square things up. I've just been called for watcho. Rolling this way and that. I looked into the after focsal and that looked like a bombed buildings with things thrown all over.

No point calling the daymen out as they can't do much today, unless of course they help the cook or take an hour on the bridge. Breakfast was a challenge for the cook with the oil filled stove backfiring and occasionally throwing fuel on to the deck. I managed to get a bacon and sausage sarnie which had been thrown into the oven door but turned out ok, although a strong presence of diesel could be tasted. I grabbed a cup of tea then proceeded to the bridge. It was quite challenging walking through the engine room with the heavy rolling, having to stop a couple of times until I reached the bridge ladders. Climbing up the ladders I lost half my pot of tea but luckily nobody was directly below me. I finally reached the bridge and put my cuppa into the pot rack. I was handed the watch by the Mate and as he was leaving the bridge asked me to keep the ship steady. 'Like you have been?' was my curt reply.

With only one bridge window open on the lee side, you could hear the wind screaming through the riggings. Portside rail kept dipping with water up to the ships rail from amidships to the stern. We are now passing the Firth of Tay and by 2100 hours we started to get a lee from the land. The Skipper came on watch and one of my watchmates went down below to make a fresh cup of tea for the Skipper and my watchmates. The teapot consisted of a spout and handle which could be easily carried. We had our own pots and just a pot for the Skipper was needed. With the weather being calmer under the land, so to speak, the Skipper decided to give us all an issue of either cigarettes or tobacco with the remainder being given out when we reached the fishing grounds. I didn't mind really as I was content getting a smoke with a few packets of cigarette papers.

Whilst we were under the land, we checked the anchor and forhold for any signs of water but thankfully the cement had held in the spurling pipe with no sign of any water in the chain locker and forhold. Just getting back from forward we made our way inside, to the accommodation with just one of my watchmates, when we hit a heavy squall. Hailstones rattled on the decks, making horrific noises. No sooner had it started it moved away, with the wind which is now coming from the southwest, making the ship now steady, in our passage to the NORTHERN WATERS.

Bloody hell!! Laid under Start Point, at anchor. The weather should be better tomorrow and we can continue with this trip. Some ships are fishing but they are not catching anything. The Skipper says that he is not chancing it. I wish that other Skippers, years ago, had taken heed but fishing is a challenge. I am going to grab a couple of hours whilst I can. We will have to wait and see what tomorrow brings. The long-range forecast says it's getting better but, as we all know, they get it wrong at times. Ask Michael Fish!

Finally, just after midnight, we have sailed out of Start Point. The seas are calmer yet we can still hear the wind as it passes through the ships rigging. I was called out just after 0300 hours to put the net over the side whilst the Mate and Skipper had been on the bridge. Firstly, the trawl doors went over the side being held by a safety chain. Next the lashings on the trawl were either cut or taken off the net. Finally, the chains that secured the bobbins from moving, were taken off. I went forward with the fore-end-men and retied the cod line. When the order was given the cod ends were heaved out on the yo-yo wire and then the order came to 'LET GO!' Quickly the belly and baiting's, followed just after by the square and wings. Shortly after the Dhan lenos were lowered into the water. With the ship on a steady course, gathering speed, we payed the doors away into the water. The order came off the bridge '250 fathoms' which indicated how much warp was required. 'Last fifty!' was then shouted by me up to the bridge. The ship then eased down in speed. A hook [called the messenger] was attached to the fore warp and the order was given by me again, to let go of the hook. This slid down the fore warp which in turn picked up the after warp into a large block with a heavy hinge which contained both the wires. It was then released and taken off. The shout came from aft 'ALL SQUARE' and we were now fishing once more.

Over the last couple of days, we have averaged just over 250 kits of fish (10stone = 1 kit) of mostly large cod. We have found a spot with not another boat in sight. We have had the odd coley but nothing like we did last month. Most of the fish have roes and chicklings as March is the spawning season. The Cook had boiled a few then fried some for a breakfast side dish. With salt and pepper, it brings out a terrific taste. Please don't knock it until you have tried it.

We have done a little damage to the nets on occasions, mostly belly heads, with catching a few boulders. We will dump these over the rough grounds when we get the opportunity. This time of year, it is just starting to warm up a little, although gales of wind can soon appear. We never take anything for granted. We have been doing three and sometimes four-hour tows which, on occasions, gives us a bit of spare time where we can play card games like crash or cribbage or even dominoes. Most tend to read cowboy or war yarns and I've always made sure that I had two or three pairs of cod ends made up and this is what I did if I was not required on the bridge, as well as any small parts of the net. There's one thing that we never do and that is get bored. Every day is a challenge. Yes, we do have our off days but generally we just get on with things and hopefully reap the rewards with a decent catch but most of all, we come home safely.

I have just eaten a lovely Sunday roast beef dinner with mashed and roast potato, carrots, with the last of the savoy cabbage, with a plain steamed duff either for dinner or dessert. I chose dessert with treacle and custard. I am wishing now that I hadn't eaten so much, as we have just become fast on the seabed. I am now putting my waterproofs on and I'm either burping or belching. As I'm finally putting on my thigh boots, just stepping out of the after-door way, when the ship lurched to starboard and the obstruction on the sea bed was now clear.

I'm standing at the winch controls, the after door comes up without a problem but when the fore door came up the weighted shoe had come clear of the wooden structure, therefore a new trawl door is REQUIRED. Luckily the rest of the net had been ok with about 100 baskets of large cod. After we had the net aboard and thankfully the weather had been like a milk pond. We managed to undo the backstraps which we attached to the door and in turn let us spread the net out, as we pulled it along. We dodged a couple of miles to a rough ground area and dumped the old door over the side. We then turned to the spare door on the port foredeck and attached the backstraps to it. Next, we pulled the warp off taking it over the whaleback. This was then attached to the new door and linkages. With the Gilson passed under the spare door and attaching a shackle to the ships rail, we slowly heaved. When things were ideal, we put the warp ends over the side, making sure they were not on the anchor flues. We then heaved, until the trawl door went over the rail. We then heaved onto the warp and now we are back in business. No more big meals for me during the day from now on!

Feeling quite gutted, hence the quote, that we are now approaching the lock gates after finishing yet another voyage to the westward fishing grounds. I have really enjoyed my time here but now I have to go to pastures new, as when I came here, I had been relieving the other thirdhand who had been at college sitting his mates' ticket. Now he wants his place back. Looking back on this trip, we lost a couple of days through bad weather. Now we are 16 days with 1,250 kits of fish which is nearly 50/50% cod and haddock, with 40kits mixed and rough fish. We averaged 120 kit a day which seems a decent living. Not too much mending, the odd belly out and changed the fore door.

On one occasion we were fishing just off the land at Eshaness and this is where we caught the haddocks. We also picked up a dead seal carcass but we did not realise until we were at the rail pulling in the net and had a whiff of something decaying. The reality had been that when the cod ends came in with about ten baskets of fish, the cod ends hit the bag ropes and then dead meat with bone splashed all over the foredeck. We had to chuck the fish and carcass etc over the side and wash the decks down but the smell lingered for days. Those that have picked whalebones up etc. when at Iceland will know what I mean. We are now through the lock gates and just finished tying up to the fish quay. My final job had been to leave the wheel amidships where I had been given a bottle of whiskey. The Skipper shook my hand and said thank you. I often see Derek and sometime his first wife and as I've said previously with other fishermen, we became friends for life.

10

Ross Jackal

Just been down dock for my liver money (fish oil) and signed on the log book with the Skipper, Lenny Smith and the Mate Glen Cunno. I am 3rd hand, Jack Quantrill is fish room man with Deck Hands Keith Hopkins, John Foster, Dave Pratt, Tommy Fisher, Donzo Ward, the cook John Watson and Jim Dunks, 2nd engineer unfortunately the others names seem to escape me.

Not too bad though for remembering names from over 40 odd years ago but sadly, not all of them are still with us but their memories are and hopefully these stories keep our Fishing Heritage ALIVE.

Sailing Monday and we are ordered for 0300 hours. My kitbag has been packed and put in the cupboard under the stairs. As it's a Saturday night, aunty who lived next door to us, would babysit the children for us whilst we went out. Firstly, to the Clee Park to meet up with Tommy and Michelle Fisher who were usually in the bar. Nearly all the same faces were in there every night not just at weekends. I wish I could afford to do this but bills have to be paid first. We usually had a couple of pints in the bar. Then a taxi to Cleethorpes to the usual haunts, Vic [Victoria Hotel], Submarine, Dolphin and depending on what was on at Bunny's or to the Winter Gardens but we always enjoyed the company of Tom and Michelle.

I never had much love and attention growing up. My mother gave me lots of love in my younger years but losing her at the early age of ten made me feel unloved. I didn't feel I had the love that I needed in my youth. Usual thing of knocking about in gangs and getting into petty mischief. Looking back, all I really needed was stability in my life. Eventually my nana came to live with us and things got better. Then my father met and married a woman who had been a social worker, who didn't like children.

I came home from sea to find an empty house with my father waiting to say that he was getting married and that I was not welcome to live with them. The house we had lived in had been given up and the contract ended. Talk about feeling unwanted but help came when I moved in with my grandmother at her sisters until nana had her own council flat for me and her. Two trips later both my two brothers and sister moved in with us. That meant five people in a two bedroomed flat. Not long after they moved out finding partners of their own.

My elder brother had still been living at my nan's when I met Cheryl and my life changed for the better. Having children of our own, a mortgage for our house, where stability and love returned to my life. We have now been married for over 50 years. We've had our ups and downs, happiness and tragedies but most of all a close extended family in which we share our problems when needed. Family life is so important to me. My childhood made me stronger to become the person that I am today.

I was in the taxi with Uggy (Jack Quantrill) and he was talking about pissing horse racing again. That's all I needed! I never liked leaving the wife and family which seems to get harder now that the children are growing up. It was early morning and a few people were staggering home from a party or a night out. We soon arrived on the North Wall, getting out the taxi, then climbing up a ladder and over the Whaleback with my gear over my shoulder. I no longer had the typical kitbag with its long handle. I now have a holdall which lets me carry extra things without being bulky. Sizer had been on the quayside but I ignored him. A couple of trips ago he asked if I wanted a lift off the dock as he was going back to the rank at Riby Square. I thanked him and got inside and he then took me to the rank. He then tried to charge me and I told him basically to 'piss off' but stronger words.

Going down below I met the Mate who I've never sailed with before. He went by the name 'Cunno' and we seemed to hit it off together. I knew his brother John better than him, from the Clee Park. The 2nd engineer had been a friend of the cooks and they shared a cabin which meant that I had a two-man cabin to myself. The Chief Engineer had not happy but I was and that's all that mattered to me.

I popped on the quayside to get some gutting gloves where the Skipper had just been getting out of his car. I said hello to his wife Doreen, who I knew from my wife's side, as she had once been married to Cheryl's uncle. Back up the ladder as the crew were coming forward to let go. I dashed to my cabin, put my things in a locker, then onto the bridge, steering her out of the dock and down the river Humber.

First night steaming towards the fishing ground. Just after tea and a few lights ahead depicted some inshore boats heading towards Scarborough with their catches of fish or crabs to sell. I am now standing behind the ships wheel and after I had put the ships position down and filled in the radio log. It is just under an hour since we sailed and I am standing here with a fresh mug of tea which my watchmate had just made.

Uggy and my other watch mate, Big Jerry Proudlove, who had asked to go on my watch with me and nobody questioned why. Some people didn't know how to take Jerry but I seemed to get one well with him and had no issues. With eventide the lights stood out from the coast, with the red and green lights of vessels plying their trade. Radio Luxembourg could be heard in the background, playing the latest releases. Such as The Bee Gees, Olivia Newton-John, George Harrison, My Sweet Lord etc. Uggy kept mentioning horses and working at Jeff Carlsberg's bookies. I had no interest, as horse racing is one subject I never understood and still don't to this day.

The Bridge of a Cat Boat

We passed one of our ships heading for tomorrow's market. They told us that there was a bit of fish being caught on the east coast of the Shetland Isles but it was small whiting's. This was regarded as prison and hospital food and not a fish as nice as haddock. In later years I changed my opinion when I was not too picky about what fish I was given from a few lads who had work in later years when things became even worse for us fisherman.

A few of the herring gulls were flying just past the starboard bridge windows being lit up by the odd sidelights that we displayed. Peeping astern the phosphorus had been lighting up the wash being given out from our propellers. Away from the land the skies were lit up with a multitude of stars. The occasional shooting star made me wonder where the meteorite would land.

It soon came to the end of the watch which I handed over giving the last known position, saying that the night orders were in the book. I signed off the radio log with nothing to report. I made my way down towards the galley and helped myself to a nice cheese sarnie with a coating of strawberry jam and a half pot of tea and made my way to my cabin. I took my gear off, read for a while and soon sleep overcame me, with the thumping of the pistons and a gentle roll to port then starboard. I thought of home and hoped that we would catch a decent trip.

At 0700 hours I was called out for breakfast which I enjoyed. My belly full of kippers, with just a couple of fresh busters spread with echo margarine which dribbled from the corner of my mouth, I washed it all down with a fresh pot of tea. The only bad part had been the size of the tea leaves which were similar to three leaved clover and not forgetting the broken stalks. At least it kept us warm.

At 0730 hours I went on the bridge to relieve the Mate. Both he and the Skipper went down for brekkie together. We were just coming up to the 'granite city' which is Aberdeen and all was quiet. The fishing boats did not leave the port until 1100 hours which seemed to be a ruling made by crews and the union. We didn't have a union in Grimsby and I remember a couple tried to set one up and another where you paid your subs in the pubs.

We are only three miles outside the harbour and we could make out the grey buildings and houses in the background plus many oil supply boats with bright colours entering and leaving the harbour bringing food, stores and supplies to and from the rigs. Where the rigs are now situated, they had once been prominent fishing grounds and vessels are now having to find new areas to catch fish.

Just after 0800 hours the Skipper came on to the bridge saying I could go down on the deck with the daymen. Leaving Jerry and Uggy on the bridge I made my way to my cabin and changed into my deck gear with my gutting knife. I made my way onto the main deck. The seas are calm and I went to the whaleback area, looked inside and went down the fore hold to familiarised myself with where things were stored. There were a few spare parts made up; top wings, lower wings, floats made up on line, two full cod ends, both with new cod line meshes applied.

Luckily for me the trawl had been overhauled going home and the spare trawl on the portside didn't need any attention. 0930 hours [ish], we went aft, had a fresh pot of tea and a couple of smokes until we returned back on to the deck. Sometime before lunch the bond was issued, I took my allowance and had a nogging of rum. I let my watch mates to get theirs's whilst I took over the Helm. We were now just passing Rattary Head once again. When the afternoon watch took over, I grabbed an hour or so whilst Uggy and Ted Loftus went to prepare the fish room.

We should be reaching the fishing grounds just after lunch. Fishing watches have been set just after breakfast time. With the last of the kippers gone we are now looking forward to some fresh HADDOCK!

Just after lunch the order was given to heave the cod ends out over the side using the yoyo (For those who don't know, this is a long arm which enables us to swing the end part of the net over the side). The order was then given to 'LET GO!' Quickly the bellies pulled out. The bellies being attached to the quarter ropes and bobbins (weights) which, when told to do so, were released but not before the links were attached to the dan leno arms which enabled us to retrieve the trawl. When the order was given, they were lowered into the water. Soon we were turning to starboard where the trawl doors were lowered. On gaining speed, the ship steering on a straight course and the trawl doors were lowered to the required depth. Soon the order came from the towing block area 'All Square Aft!' One or two old fish which had been stuck in the net but finally fell on our decks, didn't smell very nice. In a couple of days or so the crew would smell the same stench.

I wasn't needed on the bridge as the Skipper was taking the tow, using the Decca plotter, going over the sheets of graph paper that gave areas were fish had been caught before and of course tell-tale areas where the nets had come fast on the seabed. All this knowledge has sadly now gone, as we will see in later stories.

The weather is good but generally the area just north of the Orkneys seems mostly overcast but on clear days we can see Fair Isle and Foula which are small islands where we sometimes would try our luck, to see if there were any descent fish to catch. I relieved the Skipper for his tea and then went for mine on his return. Whilst I was sitting having my tea I heard a gentle tap, knocking the pin out of the block, followed by a mighty thud as the block hit the ships side which we all soon became accustomed to.

Being called out at midnight with a lukewarm mug of tea which didn't taste very nice, was not the best way to wake up. The ship had hauled and shot away again by midnight, with the tea being made for hauling time. The Mate had a quick yarn with me, telling me how much fish had been caught and the amount of warp which had been used. Before he went on to the bridge to relieve the Skipper, my watchmates and I went on to the deck to clean the fish. We had about fifty baskets of cod and haddock.

As I stepped over the grating to get into my spot for gutting, thc lads had put a few tusks and ling for me to clean. I didn't take the bait and just carried on gutting without saying anything. Don Ward, who was one of the deckies said: 'Nice fish!' to me but I ignored him. Then he blurted out: 'You'll always get these types of fish seeing as your on-film star wages!' Again, I ignored him. He was standing immediately in front of me and I picked up a large ling, cut the tongue out [which always protruded from these fish], finished gutting it and took a swing to throw the fish in the washer. This hit Don on his head, knocking off his hat which went into the washer followed by the fish. It seemed strange that I didn't get many of those types of fish, well, at least for a while!

Over the last couple of days, we have been fishing east of the Shetland Isles catching a steady living of about 250 kits a day of mostly haddock with a few monkfish but mainly a good scattering of haddock. A few of the lads have had the haddock rash which was small boil like pips that become very sore but only lasted a couple of days. I had the dreaded jumbo wrist. It suddenly comes on but then quickly goes again. The Mate had to tie and release the cod line just for about twelve hours until the problem disappeared. Strange things happen at sea or so they say.

We picked up a few rotten bones from a seal or something and the lads started boking and so did I. It had been like a chain reaction. I started, then a couple of lads started but unlike the last time we had caught a similar thing, the smell soon disappeared. I could eat my dinner though, had a cuppa and a few smokes. I think Jerry told Uggy off about effing horse racing and we could see that his lip had dropped further. Pratty kept playing Mike Oldfield on his portable cassette, Tubular Bells, I seem to recall. The weather has been quite good up to now and on these types of ships we listen to a lot of local radio with, of course, the shipping forecast. We have had little or no mending. Just the odd hole in the belly now and again but nothing major.

Early morning and we arrived on The Papa Bank. Company vessels were reporting large catches of cod. We shot the net away and after just thirty minutes the ship came to a standstill and we were hard and fast with the net stuck on the seabed. The order came from the bridge to knock out and after a couple of attempts with the 'Big Hammer', the trawl warps were released from the towing block. Gradually, we took up the slack warp until the winch stopped heaving. We were now directly above the obstruction and suddenly we became free with the warps now being retrieved at full speed. Both trawl doors came up, with the dhan lenos soon following. It had been apparent that the foreword top and lower wing were missing. The cod ends surfaced with a decent number of fish and slowly but surely, working as a team, the net, with 60 baskets of large cod was heaved aboard. Luckily, we had a top and lower wing made up minus the floatation. We cut out all the strag ends that were left of the net. We then attached the new parts to the rest of the trawl and the floatation's were soon attached. Within the hour the net was back in the water.

With a quick pot of tea, we were now cleaning the fish (gutting) which meant cutting the neck off the fish, removing the intestines whilst putting the livers into a basket. Some of the crews were quicker doing this than others. The fish was then thrown in to the fish washer and the process was repeated until all the decks were clear of fish. On this occasion it took us just over an hour of gutting to clear the decks. The Mate sang out from the bridge for my watch to pop on the bridge for our nightly rum issue telling us that we had another hour or so till we haul the nets again. I told the duty watch to get a quick drink and to then start making the net replacement. Meanwhile the rest of us took our gear off and relaxed with a smoke until we were needed again. Whilst on the deck the Northern Lights gave us a fine display.

Just over a week away and we have nearly a thousand kit of fish in the fish room and it is nearly a 50/50 split of cod and haddock. I must admit that it's a great atmosphere on this ship. The Skipper, Lenny Smith, takes things in his stride, nothing seems to bother him and he is a calming influence. Meanwile, the Mate (Cunno) sometimes runs around like a headless chicken, but only on deck. When he is sitting aft with us, he will mix well with the crew. The food on here is very good (Alec Pye, cook). All the meals are tasty and varied through the week. Some cooks had set days, with shackles one day, pie the next then maybe a chicken dinner. Fish would be on every meal and not just fried, it was steamed, baked, with some doing Halibut soup. One of my favourites would either be dry ash (corned beef mixed with mashed potatoes) lathered in daddies' sauce or meat pie with the latter still being one of my favourites with fish which I still have a few times a week.

Just after lunch we hauled with a little mending. We are on hard ground and picking up small boulders, with some just damaging the belly part of the net only. Looking around there are a few of our company's ships, as well as Taylor's, [Tokyo, Erimo, Osako] just hope that we get home without flooding the market. Tea time is soon approaching. I am looking forward to having my tea and rolling in. Now starting to feel weary after the weekend we should get our docking orders. This is always a good time and it's when the smiles come back on the men's faces, knowing that we are GOING HOME!

We are having to run into Piero Wal in the Orkney islands, as whilst we were knocking out, one of the crew fell and landed awkwardly on his wrist. He seems to be in a lot of pain. We had to drop the trawl doors in and by the time we had cleared the fish, about 30 baskets, we were approaching the Harbour where the agent had been waiting for the ship to take the injured person to the local doctors. After a couple of hours, with his hand bandaged up, the crew member returned with painkillers, saying that it was only badly sprained. Within a couple of hours, we were back fishing again. The injured person stayed off the deck whilst hauling and shooting the net but he worked down the fish room clearing the fish from the stage. Within twenty-four hours he was back on full duties. We only have forty-eight hours left and the trip will be over. Just goes to show the temperament of a fishermen, no whinging and get back to the work that we had CHOSEN to do as a CAREER.

I was called out at 0245 hours for watcho. I did not often miss dropping the doors and stowing the nets. I had a quick cuppa and a couple of smokes and my watch slowly made our way to the bridge to relieve the Mate, as we are now on steaming watches. We were told that the doors and net were put away at around 2200 hours last night and decided to leave us in as all the work and fish were put away before midnight. Our rum ration had been left in the bridge pot rack for my watch mates which I dished out mid watch. We are now just passing Dennis Head and now set a course three miles off Duncansby Head. The weather is good and a few Fulmer's were following us, looking for titbits that went out of the scuppers. We could still hear the ships on the fishing grounds saying that we are going home with a decent trip of 1,350 kitts. With not much fish being landed we should make a decent trip.

Breakfast soon came upon us, with the usual thing handing the watch over with the last known position and finally signing off the radio log. Then it's down the ladders into the messdeck for a couple of fried Haddocks straight out of the frying pan. The daymen had been called and I passed on a few jobs which needed to be done. I asked to be called just before lunch. Breakfast finished, gear off and finally, yes finally, started to read my GARDENING BOOKS once more.

I was called out for lunch time, I needed a couple of smokes and a fresh mug of tea. Just after 1300 hours I took a stroll on to the deck and started pottering around. I started by giving the trawl a quick overhaul, taking out the odd fish that had been stuck in the net, throwing them over the side and I watched as the seagulls were fighting for the remnants. Just after 1700 hours I went aft for a quick shower and a change of gear before going on watch. We should be docking tomorrow with another trip over. After tea I went on watch and the Skipper went down for something to eat. We had just passed Duncansby Head with the night just drawing in. I heard in the background Wick Radio calling us on the ships radio saying that they had traffic for us. After a few minutes the Skipper came up with the news I had received. Lenny started calling Wick Radio and within five minutes contact had been made. However, the News was not what we EXPECTED.

The Skipper called me to his cabin saying that we have to stay out for another twenty-four hours as there are too many ships for the lumpers to handle. The Skipper blamed me because I had a SHOWER [ha-ha]! He said that I could be the 'grim reaper' and go to tell the rest of the crew. My two watchmates on the bridge [Uggy and Big Jerry], just shrugged their shoulders. I slowly climbed down the bridge ladders with the teapot and told to make a pot of special. Now I'm being bullied [ha-ha]. I walked through the engine room and I shouted to the chief engineer giving him the news. He said he was signing off when she docks. I popped my head in the galley where the cook was tidying up from the tea time meal. He just said 'What will be, will be!' A few of the lads, including the Mate, told me to 'eff off' saying that it was a wind up!

They knew that it wasn't when all hands were called out for shooting the net. We were at a place called 'A Hole in The Brock' which is a few miles off the Peterhead coastline. It had been a while since I had been there. We only had three hauls. The first haul we picked up a shopping trolley with a couple of baskets of mixed fish, with plenty of weed and starfish and a few hermit crabs trying to hide. The next haul was similar stuff with a few prawns included in this catch and the last haul, milk trays, an old bike etc. It must be an area where things are dumped or it seemed that way. Just after breakfast the nets were stowed once more. My watch went below and we were NOW going home at half speed and should be docking the next afternoon. Now to get some rest!

Yes, finally we are in the river Humber heading towards the lock gates. It's a great feeling, with a decent catch, as not a lot of fish has been reported for the market tomorrow. My last watch will be 0300 hours to breakfast. During our watch we had the ships brass work to clean, with all of us onboard having to clean the ship ready for docking. After the watch we had a bit of toast and a fresh cuppa. I then went to my cabin to pack my gear and grabbed an hour's sleep on my bunk.

After passing Flamborough Head mid-morning we hugging the land and could see from a distance, people walking their dogs on the beach. Others were going about their business oblivious of who we were and what we have been up to. We were just another ship passing to them, I suppose. Just ahead of us a couple of Taylor's boats were coming towards us and heading to the fishing grounds that we have just left. A couple of hours later we were coming up to Spurn Light Ship, with the last of this morning's sailings approaching us.

On coming around the Lightship we could see a couple of people with their fishing rods passing the time away and hopefully getting a fry for tea. We were soon approaching the Anchorage and the order had been to 'standby to drop the hook'. I was sent down with my watch to make things ready. Soon the anchor had been dropped which secured the ship to the seabed. We would not be lifting the anchor until 1900 hours. So frustrating to be so near to our loved ones and yet so far. We've been away just over two weeks. A few more hours will soon pass.

On landing day Uggy, (Jack Quantril) would come and let me know what we had turned out on the fish market and the average price of fish. Not forgetting, of course, bringing my fry from Johnny Lacey's. I would often give him a nogging and he would be on his why.

This time home I received a phone call from a good friend of mine, Gary Evans, saying that a position had become available for me, if I was interested, on the GRIMSBY LADY. The ship was a Purse Seiner which was a different type of fishing from that which I had been used to operating. I waited until the wife came home and discussed the job opportunity with her and was told to give it a go. The next thing I had to do was inform the trawler company B.U.T. of my intention of

giving it a go, to ensure that I left on good terms. They told me if it doesnt work out I could always come back to the company.

Random Memory

Getting out of the taxi, after travelling around for nearly an hour, as I had been picked up first, by that man Sizer. I asked him: 'Why the fuck have you picked me up first?' He replied that he knew I would be ready. My response was: 'If you pick me up first again, I won't be held responsible for the outcome!'

Stretching my legs, I looked along the North Wall seeing a number of ships tied up, nose to nose, with ladders leading up towards the whaleback. What a sad sight to see, after having a dock full of deepwater vessels not just the sidewinders. A few had gone to different countries to carry on catching fish all over the World but the majority had gone for scrap.

All the proceeds for selling and decommissioning of these vessels went to the trawler owners. Not a penny went to the Fishermen who lost their livelihoods. Lots of money went into cold stores and farming so that they could still make a profit. People fought for many years to obtain Redundancy.

When we did finally receive payment, it was a pittance, in my opinion. Plenty of fisherman did not receive a penny due to 'time served conditions' (Continued Employment) being for one firm. Many men changed companies to maintain employment when ships went into dry dock or for refits etc. It makes my blood boil, even today. Had it not been for the tenacity of certain individuals, namely Dolly Hardy, I don't think we would have received a penny. It is just my opinion but I don't believe enough credit has been given to Mrs, Hardy for all the hard work she did. A lesser person would have given up after the many obstacles which were presented by the government and trawler owners at the time. I believe it is a shameful time in our history.

Random Memory

Standing in the fish pounds for hours on end, often frozen to the bone and from the after end of the ship came the smell of fresh bread. Our taste buds would soon come alive awaiting food the food we needed to recharge our bodies. 'BREKKIE' would be screamed from the after end of the ship. On arrival aft we would take off our waterproofs, a quick use of the toilet, followed by a scrub of our hands then making our way to the messdeck. Fresh busters awaited us and we quickly grabbed one, spreading margarine inside where you had swiftly torn it apart. There could be fish be on the menu with either a full English or at the end of the trip, when food supplies started to dwindle, fish or porridge would be served. Of course, the cook couldn't please everyone but to me they were the unsung heroes. They were working in all kinds of weather and harsh conditions and the food had to be prepared daily to ensure that the ship ran smoothly. This was often done without complaint.

Random Memory

There were many great Cooks and some who were not so good in the 'Cat' boats. I always enjoyed the food prepared by John Smith, his duffs and bread. Nothing was ever too much for him and he would prepare any food stuff you fancied, if it was available.

Randon Memory

Getting called out of your pit at midnight is not my idea of FUN. Being on the grounds working Melaka, a well-known fishing area, which had been a hard ground to fish. Every other haul, either a haul of fish or a broken trawl. The crew was getting short tempered with one another. Trivial things become a 'big deal' because of the tiredness due to a lack of sleep as we were working 18 hours a day. However, we are quite fortunate as in the 50s and 60s there were no watch belows. Thankfully, at least now we do have a rest period with mealtimes and a 30-minute shout. We are lucky to have say 4 hours, in total.

The mate came into the mess telling me what was what, saying the broken trawl was repaired and when we haul, we will be steaming south to shorten the distance. We are going to the Working Man's Bank or to Hari Kari.

Sitting, looking at my hands, wrapped around a mug of tea, all the blisters and sores from this trip and with the aching limbs, oh what I would give to be laid in a Radox Bath, with clean gear and clean bedsheets to roll in to. Within a few days this would become a reality.

Oh, for the price of FISH.

Random Memories

There's no better feeling, sailing down the river, passing spurn lightship with a hold full of fish and knowing that the Markets are paying top-notch for decent fish. The skipper passes me a dram of rum which is the second one since I've been on the ships wheel.

Skipper Lenny Smith

Passing the burcom with the heading due west and now approaching the lock gates. Passing through the gates I catch the sight of my two children and Cheryl waiting by the car and I managed a wave back.

As we make our way into the fish docks the ship suddenly turns to port, counteracting the manoeuvre we are now heading towards Henderson's jetty. Soon the forward ropes are passed ashore and swiftly followed by the stern ropes. The skippers said to me; 'Wheel amidships Snowy!' and then wanders into his cabin, bringing me a bottle of spirits. As I leave the bridge, he shakes my hand bidding me farewell. Such a gentleman to sail with! Skipper Lenny Smith.

Random Memory

We had caught very little fish last haul. The skipper, Lenny smith, called me on the bridge to take the rest of the tow (being in charge of fishing over the grounds). I had taken a large mug of coffee with me and made sure that I had my baccy, cigarette papers and of course my storm lighter, making sure that it been topped with petrol. Now on the bridge, I've been given the area to be fished.

We were on Papa Bank which was notorious for breaking the nets but if the fish were there you could catch it in abundance. I had been on the Bridge for about twenty minutes when on the fish finder we came across what looked like a polo mint on the seabed. The Skipper had laid on the seat locker reading when he heard me mutter; 'What is this?' He came and looked at the fish mark and told me to call the lads out saying that we would be hauling the trawl in twenty minutes.

Thirty minutes later the order came to knock out. The winch had been shipped up and we were in full flow of hauling in the net and both trawl doors had been heaved up. The Skipper decided to take a turn out of her and as he started to turn to starboard, we could see the cod ends rise out of the water.

The bobbins came aboard then and slowly but surely, we emptied the net of fish. Seven times I had to let go of the cod ends, then retie the cod line. Nearly 400 baskets of extra-large cod, really good shifting swag. The Skipper shouted down to me; 'Do you think it's worth one?' (Dram of rum). I just nodded my head.

A few of our ships had been in the general area to us but we were the only ones who had caught this amount of fish.

That's what you call 'being in the right area at the right time'!

AFTER THE DEMISE OF THE MIDDLE WATER FISHING

One by one the Cat boats came in from sea knowing that they had sailed their last voyage to the Scottish fishing grounds. I had been in the Ross Lynx, one of the first to come home and at the time we didn't know that the lumpers [fish unloaders] were on strike. This meant that in order to save the fish that had been caught, the crews had to land their own catch.

When we docked, I went home to take my sea gear off the ship and had to return to the docks just before midnight to unload our catch for the morning market. For discharging the ship [of our catch] we were paid £30 each landing. This was sometimes more money than the crews earned for being at sea for two weeks.

I was quite fortunate as I landed a few of the ships, working alongside Paul and John Ferrand who were the stepsons of a great friend and skipper Lenny Smith, who has unfortunately now sadly passed away. The last ship to dock was the Ross Jackal which was Skippered by Lenny Smith.

A couple of trips prior to it docking I had a big fall out with Lenny and left the ship after being there a couple of years. I am pleased to say we soon became friends again with respect for each other. **I sailed with him again a few trips later.**

After landing the Jackal I went home not knowing how my life would change and how I would earn a living. All I had known was a life as a seaman.

Random Memory

During my time at sea, I have been quite fortunate, as I married the girl of my dreams and had two lovely children. Matthew is no longer with us as he was murdered in AFGHANISTAN in 2009 but the time we had with both our children has given us many HAPPY MEMORIES which will last forever.

I have sailed with some good crews and some not so good. I am not going to mention names or ships but, on some ships, if you were not in the 'inner circle', so to speak, the trips seemed to last longer and I would just want to get the trip over and sign off the ship. By law, up to 48 hours' notice had to give that you wouldn't be going back but I think when you tell the skipper on your 2nd day at sea that you would not be going back, then it would be enough notice. I hated sailing with 'rats', who as quick as a flash, would inform the skipper or mate if any bad words were spoken about them. I'm sure that I'm not the only one who can relate to this.

I've been to some great places fishing, including Iceland, the Faroes, Greenland, Barney, Spitzbergen, Jan Mayen. Murmansk (effing cold), Flemish Cap, Labrador, and a few more places which I will write about in later yarns. To see the Northern Lights should be on everyone's Bucket list, with the SOUTH FJORDS, being there also.

When we were at sea, we didn't see our children growing up so much but now that I am retired and I see most of the grandkids and now the great grand kid growing up, I realise how much I missed. I'm now a tour guide on the Ross Tiger, something I like doing very much; meeting the General public and making new friends and that is what life is all about.

Random Memory
Ross Tiger

Left to Right: Bosun, Ron Telford, Brian Bevan, RNLI (the most decorated Lifeboat Coxswain to date) and Skipper Dennis Avery

Who would have thought that over forty years ago that Dennis Avery and myself would be working back on the Ross Tiger. Not as Skipper and Thirdhand but as tour guides, taking the general public and school tours around this iconic fishing vessel.

I can remember sailing with Dennis as skipper, Dennis Picket as mate and with me being bosun. On the day that we sailed I had been summoned to the bridge to steer the vessel out of the dock and towards Spurn Light vessel. I can clearly remember coming off the bridge and meeting Danny

Morris, his brother Tom and George Davis, who I had sailed with before. His wife Rose worked at the Seamans' Mission and she always smoked Capstan Full Strength cigarettes. When I was once in her company she asked if I wanted to try one. I said OK, I will try one which I did. I wish that I hadn't as I nearly coughed my lungs up. I never asked for another of her cigarettes.

I also recall another deckie called Bingo Watson who was a great shipmate, who just seemed to get on with things. I believe the cook was either John Smith or young Watto. Both were great cooks, who knew how to keep crews well fed with plenty of decent meals.

We were fishing mainly around the Shetland and the Orkney islands and we made plenty of money and always kept a good crew. Dennis had been the Skipper on the Tiger for over eight years. The mate, Dennis Picket, like me had come into these types of ships with the demise of the deep-water fishing industry. He was a very good net man and a very good friend to my late brother-in-law, Colin Quickfall. Sadly, they are both no longer with us.

A few months late, for some reason, Dennis came out of the Tiger and came mate with us on the Ross Jackal with Lenny Smith. I remember we had been laid mending when Dennis said to me that it's hard work on the deck doing all the manual work after being on the bridge as master for all those years. He was soon back in command of a ship and then when the catboat's finished he went skipper of smaller boat working once again in the Scottish waters.

11

Grimsby Lady

I have just been down dock and have taken all my gear off. I am now putting it in to storage until I get new orders to join the Grimsby Lady. On landing day and we made £28,000 which means that I had a decent pickup. Later that day I went to see the ships runner, Bill Batty, to sign off the 'Ships Articles'. He was not too happy but said that if things didn't work out to give him a call.

I met the wife at lunch time and I had a few pints then went home. All the time I was asking myself whether I was doing the right thing by signing off a decent ship, with a good crew. Time would tell, I suppose.

Later in the afternoon I received a telephone call from a Mr Swain, asking me to meet up with him in the morning at his workplace which was a portacabin based in Tyson's Yard. He told me to bring my P45 which had details of my earnings and tax codes, which is what I did. After school was out, I went out with the wife and children for tea to Steel's Restaurant. When we arrived back home, I thought; 'Here comes another chapter in my life!'

The day was nearly upon us when I joined as a crew member on a new adventure. I had done different types of fishing including Deep Water, Middle Water, Seine Net, Stern Trawling and now Purse Seining. I was asked if I needed a taxi to Hull which was where she was berthing or did, I have my own means of transport? I told them that the wife would drive me, when the time came.

I could not stop thinking; 'Am I doing the right thing? Am I going to better myself or am I going to wish that I kept in the boats, earning a steady living?'

We were ordered to join the ship between 12 noon and 1300 hours. I got up at breakfast time and said goodbye to the kids. I always told them that I loved them and that I would see them both soon. We left our house just after ten o'clock to travel to Hull to join the Grimsby Lady.

I had no idea what she looked like and was only told where she was berthed. After a steady drive we arrived at our destination and I was surprised at how big and mighty a ship she was, berthed alongside the quay. On getting out of our car I had been met by both Ray and Garry Evans who welcomed me helping me to bring my gear aboard and showing me to my cabin. I think that Cheryl came aboard to have a quick look around and to have a cuppa before she returned home.

I said my goodbyes to Cheryl and then familiarised myself with the ship. I was then introduced to the crew who were mostly Faroese. This meant that Ray was Flag Skipper, Garry and Pete Almond were both mate and I signed on as 2nd mate.

I was given a tour of the bridge where I met the Faroese Skipper, Agga Gardidtova, and his brother-in-law Sverry, who was mate. A few of the crew were related in one way or another. Officer's cabins were all single berths, mine was also a single, whilst the rest were double cabins. I received a few strange looks from the crew but I'm sure that I will soon overcome 'the new boy feeling' and will hopefully settle down.

The Grimsby Lady had all the modern conveniences well before her time. Most crew members had their own cabin and we carried a crew of seventeen, five of whom were English men meaning the rest of the crew (twelve) were Faroese. She had a sauna and steam room, three showers, two of which were for daily showers with the other set aside for the sauna and steam room, as it had ice cold water.

The galley had all the modern equipment with an extra-large frying pan on gimbles which were ideal to use in any foul weather (ship rolling etc,). There was an electric bread dough machine which could also be used for making fairy cakes or duffs etc. The kitchen was fitted with a dish washer, potato peeler and a large double sink. There was a changing room just to the side of the galley which also led us into the saloon which had two large TVs placed one above the other for the crew's entertainment. There were deep red plush suites and two times bench tables with seating for ten men at each table (i.e., twenty men). The cook had originally been Faroese and he provided some great meals. Although he didn't stay too long because I believe he had lady troubles and she didn't want him to go to sea.

There were two flights of stairs with the first flight to the crew's accommodation The top-level lead to the bridge which also had a toilet just on the port side aft. On the bridge there was state of the art navigation which was a Loran C. There were three sonars two of them were Wesmar's but I cannot remember the name of the other one, as it has slipped my mind for now. She had had a pilot style steering wheel, with an Arcos steering motor. There were two large fish finders which were built in Norway and I think they were Simrad. Three chairs ran on tracks so a crew member could sit alongside the sonars or the radars when we were steaming. There were also coffee making machines with biscuits provided for a snack.

Just after lunch a few of the crew ventured ashore which gave me the opportunity to put my gear away and grab an hour before we sailed but I shouldn't have worried as we were not sailing until lunchtime the following day.

After a good night's sleep, I had a wash and a smoke then ventured to the messdeck. I noticed one table had been full with the Faroese crew and the other table had been for the rest of the crew. On our table there was a bowl with a few boiled eggs, another had bacon and frankfurter sausages, placed alongside fresh bread or toast. It was a hearty breakfast with fresh coffee made very strong just the way that I made mine at home. I spoke to the wife last night saying that I felt comfortable here but maybe the language barrier would be a problem. In fact, that was not the case, as I soon found out that most of the Faroese spoke excellent English [although some better than others].

After breakfast the Faroese Mate took me around the deck explaining things that I would have to do whilst on board. The type of fishing that we would be using this trip would be a net drum and that we would be 'pelagacing' for blue whiting. 'Pelagic' means that we can adjust the net to various depths to catch fish, on the seabed, midwater depths, etc. I was then shown the net bin which contained the 'purse net' which he said he would explain better when we were on the bridge, when we both had a bit of spare time.

I noticed that on the ships funnel it had been painted with a British flag alongside a Norwegian and a Danish flag which I was informed gave us rights to fish in those waters as we were part owned by the flag countries that we displayed. It was nearly midmorning and we went back in the messdeck area. To get to the messdeck area we had to walk through a changing area, as no work gear was allowed in any of the messes.

I am now sitting with the Mate on the main crews table and he introduced me to most of the men that I had not met yesterday and as we got talking about things in general and the ships and type of fishing I had done, it seemed to break the ice. I was offered cigarettes and given more coffee. That didn't take long. Only 12 hours on board and I felt accepted.

Whilst chatting at the table I told them that whilst in the Boston Kestrel we had been taking a crew member, who had been acting very strange and could have been a danger to himself and the Skipper decided to put the man ashore in Torshavn. We were going down what we thought had been straight fjord but in actual fact it had been a dead-end fjord, so to speak and we ended up ashore, on the rocks. The locals came out in a rowing boat, took our warp ashore and after a couple of hours when the tide started to rise, we heaved ourselves clear. The man in the rowing boat had been Sverry's father, the Faroese mate. I thought how strange that his father came on board and piloted us to Torshavn. The ship had a diver look at the bottom of our ship. Fortunately, we had sustained no damage and we soon sailed on towards the fishing grounds at Iceland. We didn't make much money and I seem to remember Dave Sherrif had been the relieving skipper whilst Derek Brown had time off.

Sverry, the mate took me around the working deck. The first thing that I was shown was the net drum which seemed massive. At the bottom of the net were steel metal rings which covered the opening of the cod ends. Alongside were two sets of anchor chains used for weight on the bottom end of the trawl. At the stern were two massive pelagic doors which were made fast with chains. On the aft gantry were two large rollers for the net sensors and transducers. On the starboard quarter there was a net bin holding the purse net. Above this laid a large arm with a roller used for replacing the net in the bin. Just foreside lay a steel arm with fifty large steel rings which had lines attached to the purse.

Moving a little further on the starboard side there was a large triple block which, when used, works with both types of fishing nets. Moving further forward there were seven rows of tanks for holding the fish such as 1,200 ton of blue whiting or 800 tons of mackerel or herring. A large tank on the main deck which had steel chutes to direct the fish into the tanks. Just on the foredeck there was a large crane which was used for discharging mackerel, herring, stores etc. and any other use when it was needed. On the foredeck stood a windlass and alongside, another winch, used in connection with the purse net. A large net store was situated under the whaleback which including a lathe in the event that it was needed for the deck machinery repair. Stepping back into the accommodation, taking our working gear off and now going to have a strong coffee complete with cake or biscuits. Now I'm looking forward to sailing.

'Let go forward! Let go aft!' came the cry over the tannoid system. We began pulling the headropes and springs in. This had been made easy as the ropes were on a large reel. You just turned the handles and the ropes went around the barrel.

Two tugs took our head and stern ropes to pull us across the dock, so that we could put fuel and water into our tanks. Once we tied up, George Herds lorry had been waiting for us to replenish our food stores. Quite a few boxes came aboard of things such as milk, bread, cheeses, together with numerous other things, too numerous to mention. We also had some Bond of smokes but no alcohol. There was even soap and a few tins of Quality Street. The Customs Officer had been aboard to make sure it was locked away. Within an hour or so things settled down and we all went about our business. The Faroese crew gave me some of their gardening magazines to read, although I couldn't read any Danish but I'm sure I'll be able to INTERACT.

I am glad that we are not out there as all the ships are laid in HEAVY weather.

That's the engines all fired up, not sailing till after two which will be high water, then the tide turns to take us down the river. Fuel economy. Let go forward and aft. Ropes pulled in and coiled away on the reels which are now covered and fastened down. The spring rope had been passed to one of two tugs which slowly pulled us away from the quayside towards the bullhead of the lock gates.

Gradually we were through the gates and very soon under our own power. A few people going about their daily business gave us a wave and some saying; 'Have safe trip!' Looking forward to being at sea, a new venture let's see how this goes.

Grimsby and Hull, over the years, have had men sail from both ports who were never to return but such is the occupational perils that go with our profession which is considered one of the most dangerous jobs in the world. Behind us we can see the Humber Bridge linking Lincolnshire and Yorkshire via the river Humber. Ten minutes at half speed and we could feel the thrust of the engines as the speed soon reached 15 knots. On our portside we are passing the P O Ferry Terminal whilst on the opposite side we are coming up to the oil refineries of Immingham which is a port that is steadily building up with plenty of cargo and container vessels now using this port.

As we are hugging the Lincolnshire coast line, we are soon seeing the Dock Tower standing majestically between the two docks of commercial and fish. Everything on the decks have been secured for sea and we are all ship shaped and Bristol fashion. All water tight doors are now closed. I was been called on the bridge to go on watch with Ray who would show me the ropes prior to taking a watch. In just under the hour, we were coming around the Lightship heading North.

0400 hours and we finally reached the fishing grounds. We are SW off the Irish Coast and all hands have been called out to shoot the net. We have a crew of fifteen plus two skippers, one being Raymond Evans and the other being Agga Gardidtova who is the Faroese skipper.

I take up my position working portside aft. We have three men each side working the afterdeck. The cod line is threaded through and made secure. Two large bow shackles are connected to the four salvage eyes. The order soon came to heave the net out. The net roller reversed the net and then the out hauler had the end of the net hung out on a small hook. The order came to let go and the net roller started to pay the net away. The floats went over and after we had attached the transducer cable which had cables running down the net to the cod ends called clevis. This let us know the quantity of fish that went into the net. The bellies etc. soon followed and we attached the anchor chain weights to the gear. Soon the linkages were attached to the trawl doors, being lowered to the require depth. Breakfast time soon arrived which was a large bowl of boiled eggs, platters of bacon with fresh bread to wrap it all in. There were cereals if preferred. I popped on to the bridge to see how things are going and it was like nothing I had ever seen before with all the modern systems being used. On the ships I had previously sailed there were only primitive sounders and plotters.

I am going to grab a nap while I can and look forward to hauling time.

'THUD, THUD' came the sound of the hydraulic motors being started which startled me, as I had been laid down in my cabin. I quickly made my way out of my cabin and into the changing room where I saw Garry Evans. He was grinning at me, telling me to chill-out. With blue whiting you have to decompress the fish in the net otherwise you could damage the net. I went into the messroom and had a strong black coffee. The hydraulics came on again and heaved a few more fathoms of warp in. The controls were on the bridge which made things easier all round. This procedure kept happening for nearly two hours before the order came and we are now hauling the net.

I put my wet gear on and had a quick smoke before I ventured onto the deck. The hydraulic motors were in full flow and very soon the trawl doors appeared. The doors seemed to pull us astern and then settled down to where the chains were put on to stop any movement. The 'G link' was then unclipped and we started heaving on the pennants. After a while the anchor chain weights came onto the deck where these were taken off the bridles. A quick glance astern and the fish in the net had come to the surface.

What a sight that was! Now the seagulls started eating what they could, pulling them out of the net with their mighty beaks. The bottom part of the trawl came inboard followed by the floats. The transducer box and cable were then disconnected and put aside until we shot the net again. Slowly heaving the net, we had a piece of rope attached to a 'C link' leading to the cod ends. A line from the forward winch pulled the net onboard. We attached a large hose to the cod ends which was then put over the side to pump the fish onboard. A bight of net was put into the triple block and we then started pumping the fish onboard through a sort of large washing machine which had chutes running into separate tanks. I asked the mate (Sverry) how much fish did he reckon we had caught and he replied '500 ton!'.

After just over three hours the fish had been pumped aboard and the net released from both the pump then out of the triplex block. The net was then heaved up onto the net drum where the fish bag was tied with the large bow shackles which were put in place holding the four salvages together. The order was given to put the net in the water again and whilst reversing the net off we reconnected the line to the fish bag via a 'C link'. Soon the transducer was fitted to the headline, followed by the anchor chain weights. The pennants were lowered and attached to the trawl doors which were soon lowered into the water. Now we are fishing again. We will be hauling the net just after tea so now it's time to relax once more. I was feeling strange as there were no fish to clean. All the fish went into tanks where the water had been drained to give us more space to put in the blue whiting. We have the capacity to hold 1,500 ton. After a quick snack I was called on to the bridge to look at how the sounders and sonars enabled us to catch fish.

After we shot the net, I had been called on to the bridge by the Faroese Skipper who sat me in the bridge chair to take the tow, with a multi coloured fish finders and two times Wismar sonars working in unison, letting us know where the fish were together with the density of the shoal. Talk about being nervous! I was now left on the bridge, all by myself, whilst Agga (Skipper) had time out in the crew's mess. The best marks were at 100 fathoms in, which our net was set to and we were on a north-western heading. I took a coffee from the bridge coffee machine and it had been like tasting mud and I could have stood my spoon up it was so strong. Twenty minutes later Agga came back. He told me to go to the hydraulic controls where he showed me how to heave and lower on the net drum using the hydraulics. I have been on the ship less than a week and I had been taught how to use the bridge equipment. When I went into the messdeck the Faroese crew said 'Well done!' We hauled just after tea with another 400 ton. After the fish had all been pumped aboard, we are now destined for Skagen in the north of Denmark to discharge our cargo. I think I'm enjoying this type of work!

With nearly 900 ton of blue whiting, we are now steaming towards Skagen in Denmark. The ship has sliced through the water in heavy weather but now becoming calmer as we are approaching the Harbour. Last night we passed a few liners or cruise vessels setting fireworks off and what looked like Christmas lights flashing away on the upper decks with music being played. We are in the Skagerrak, which is the gateway to Sweden, Finland on to the Denmark straight which leads to the Baltic states. At Midnight we sounded the ships whistle and, in the distance, we could hear others doing the same.

Just after breakfast we had tied up alongside in Skagen which seemed a decent port. We are alongside a quay which smells like a fishmeal plant. All ropes are made secure and The Customs and Immigration Officers come on board and gave us clearance. No sooner had they both departed than our agent came on board, Jens Berg, who had his office in Hershels. Seemed a nice person and I was proved right in later stories. Within the hour we had taken all the hatches off, with the shore gang coming on board to discharge us using a large tube which sucked the fish out. When the suction stopped, men would go into the tanks shovelling the remnants up. These were then sucked up and when the tanks became empty, water was pumped into tanks to keep the ship stable. Mid-morning the local chandler came on board enquiring about fresh stores, etc. Two other persons came onboard with trays of Danish pastries, both trying to compete by giving us supplies.

Mid-morning, I went for a walk along the quay and noticed that a few small boats had come in with deck loads of sprats waiting to be discharged. Just ahead of us lay the St Loman which was a Hull registered purser. She was slightly longer than us with the same arrangement of fishing skipper and part English Crew. At the end of the quay had been a few shops selling marine gear etc. with a couple of Cafes and Snack. Bars. There were a few people taking a stroll around the harbour who either said 'good morgen' or just smiled as I passed them by. Just after midnight we had sailed. Now bound for Hirtshals to pick up the purse net in readiness for when we change fishing methods.

Just after breakfast we had finished tying the ship up in Hirtshals in a similar way to the North Wall. Crews on the quayside were either mending their nets or getting ready for sailing. No sooner had we tied up when the Grocer came on board with cakes and pastries. No wonder I piled on weight, well that is my excuse. The mate Sverry summoned me to the after deck and explained that we are putting the warp ends ashore to have them replaced. We lowering the trawl doors onto the chains and undid the bow shackles. We then pulled the warp ends ashore with the job completed within 30 minutes or so. We all then went for breakfast which was boiled eggs, bacon with hashbrowns.

Ray had been busy getting all the paperwork sorted after landing yesterday. We had landed just under 900 ton selling at £50 ton so not a bad week's work. Mid-morning, I had a look around the quayside and noticed a tractor coming towards us. He stopped alongside the 'Lady' picking up the warp ends and cutting about a fathom off each end. On the back of the tractor was a vice which clamped the warp end attached to a bar. After a few turns on levers, the wire had been opened, making it easy to wire splice. A simply, ingenious, bit of gear. By now it was lunchtime and I grabbed a couple of hours kip.

Mid-afternoon I went ashore and there were plenty of purse seiners in dock, mostly owned by a guy call Esperion, who apparently had 10 or more ships. On returning to the ship, I noticed that the purse net was being put onboard the ship. The mate told me that he didn't need me as enough people were in place to put it away. I stood on the quay watching the net being flaked out. Big metal rings were being put on a bar, whilst the floats were being separated from the weights in the net bin. I had been informed that we will not be going to sea until tomorrow and I've been invited ashore with the Skipper and Crew. Ray and Garry never went for a drink and gave me the ok to enjoy myself. I didn't need much persuading.

Having had a nice hot shower and a change of gear, I made my way off the gangway and teamed up with the crew mates. I seemed to have come a long way in a week both working with the Faroese and now having leisure time. The language barrier is such a problem and of course I'm learning all the swear words first. We soon arrived in a local tavern, drinking lager out of bottles. We had only been in the pub for about ten minutes when the mate came in. He gave the crew an envelope each saying it was the landing money divided between the crew. We all had an equal share. I felt better now that I had some of my own money to spend [Danish Kroners], although I didn't have to buy a drink, I felt better having my own monies. I would never go into a pub at home if I didn't have any money of my own, although I knew a few people who would.

After a few drinks we moved onto another ale house but this one was called the SKIPERKRONE. It had loud music with plenty of fishermen. It was similar to Cottee's in its heyday. Our skipper sat surrounded by other skippers and crewmates. The beer was flowing freely, then the snaps came out and a few dancing girls came in, plying their trade. The bar staff didn't get a wage and were paid on how many bottles tops he or she sold each evening. A few Norwegians had travelled from Christiansen by ferry on their journey to Europe and beyond. Just after 2300 hours I decided to make my way back to the ship.

Both Ray and Garry were in the mess deck and they asked if I had had a good time. I just said OK. I then asked Ray if I could use the ships radio to call home. No mobiles then. I had a call saying I had settled in and had been for a walk ashore and had a couple of pints. The wife said; 'JUST TWO?' lol! Just after mid-morning we let go of the ropes and courses were set back to the fishing grounds.

Having left Hirtshals just over 48 hours ago we are now back at the fishing grounds. SW of the Irish coast. Sailing day and I must admit to feeling slightly hungover. I decided to have a sauna and sweat it out of me. With my head pounding I entered the sauna and threw a bucket of water over the coals and retreated to the wooden gratings. Sitting on a towel I tried to relax. Within minutes I had to vacate the room as it became unbearable to remain. I went straight under the cold shower which took my breath away, as the shower had been linked up to a refrigeration pipe. The hangover quickly disappeared. This was my first experience of using a sauna but I soon became used to it. Lesson learned, so to speak!

As we are now on the fishing grounds with a few ships in our area, mainly Danish and Norwegian boats in search for blue whiting. Just after 0600 hours the nets were lowered into the sea. Transducer attached soon with the anchor chains (weights) attached once more and the doors lowered and we were back fishing again. I grabbed an hour as I had been on the steaming watch which took us to the fishing grounds. I managed a couple of hours as when the winch hydraulics started up, I climbed out of my bunk.

One of the lads came to my cabin saying that we had a problem with the net and we are now hauling the net straight away. I had a quick smoke, a large coffee, put my wet gear on and then went onto the deck. We had 400 fathoms of warp out which started to build up on the winch barrel. I had been told that the transducers were giving off false readings which was why we were hauling. The weather conditions were quite reasonable and we only had a hundred fathoms to heave in when from a distance we could see the trawl doors and by this time we were being pulled astern. All of a sudden, the cod ends appeared and shot out of the water with the end of the cod ends exploding and all the fish spewing out of the net. Slowly but surely things settled down we retrieved the doors, unshackled the weights and then started to retrieve the net on the net drum. When the cod ends came on to the main deck both the bow shackles had parted and a large tear was apparent in the netting. Of course, we quickly repaired the net.

Whist we were mending, the skipper came down and apologised saying the transducer and clevis attachments stated that the nets were full but he took it on to himself as he believed that the equipment had a malfunction which wasn't the case. Even the professionals admit to making mistakes. We estimated that we had caught 400 ton in a two hours tow. Within two hauls we were once more steaming to Skagen to discharge the catch again. This time a thousand ton and not one fish needing gutting as the blue whiting was bound for the fishmeal plant.

We are now back on the fishing grounds and it is the second haul of the day. We are now off the Outer Hebrides, as the fish moved to Northern waters. The first haul we caught just over 500 ton of blue whiting. It's now just after

1500 hours and we are in the process of hauling. Heaving a little on the warps and stopping, then repeating the process. By 1600 hours the trawl doors had been secured and we are now heaving on the Net Drum. Slowly but surely, we are bringing the net in. Weights are removed with the floats turning on the drum. Not so much fish, about 3 to 400 ton. As we are heaving the net in the weather is a westerly 5/6. We noticed that we had a couple of turns in the belly with the rope to the cod ends being constricted. The C link had been unclipped with a turn taken out with one more turn remaining. One of the English crew, without being named, lent across the belly to try and pass the turn clear. At this time the belly went slack and then tight again, launching the unnamed person about 20ft into the air and over the stern and into the water.

The person then climbed on top of the belly. The line became clear and we then heaved on it and the man had been able to climb over the ships rail. As the time of year meant that the waters were getting warmer, the person involved had been one lucky guy. If it had been colder or in a normal fishing boat, things may have turned out differently. Someone had been looking over him that day. Back on the ship he had a quick cup of sweet tea, a warm shower and he was back on the deck just laughing about the incident.

We landed the catch in Skagen with 850 ton. We sailed just after midnight. Reports are coming through that the fish have started to go deeper than the 100 fathoms and dispersing. Maybe we will get one more go at them before the season ends.

Whilst on the Grimsby Lady, the cook we had, previously worked in hotels in both Faroe and Denmark. He went by the name of Shorer. He cooked both English meals as well as traditional foods for the Faroese crew from their homeland. I used to eat the wind dried fish and I have eaten whale meat and chewed the blubber which had a similar texture to salted beef. I got used to these 'delicacies' as time went by but there was no way I would eat the rass fish. It smelt like rotten fish done in a soup like mixture. We could tell when this was being cooked as it stank the ship out. I used to get my own back by having kippers for breakfast.

After 48 hours steaming, we are now NW, off the Butt of Lewis still working towards the NNE following the 100-fathom line. We have had one haul with 300 ton with the trawl being in the water for over 8 hours. Today we went deeper, touching the seabed and sustaining damage to the net. As it almost impossible to repair the net at sea, it was decided to go to Torshavn and get the net repaired.

Firstly, the catch was unloaded and then we tied up stern to on the quay. Next the net was pulled off by a Land Rover and stretched along the Quay. The decision was made that the Faroese crew could have time ashore with their loved ones whilst four of us would repair the net which only took about four hours to repair. The net was heaved back on the Net Drum and the ship was now tied up alongside the Smyrll which was a passenger/cargo vessel running from Aberdeen/ Kirkwall/Faroe Islands then onto Iceland. Within three hours of docking, she had left Torshavn to continue her journey.

As most of the crew were ashore, I had been delegated as cook. The regular cook, who had gone home, had left food in the fridge that just needed cooking. I seem to remember that we didn't starve. I think that I cooked a mixed grill. After tea one of the engineers came onboard with his wife, staying onboard to keep an eye on the generator.

In the evening I went on the quayside where a few people were fishing, catching Sul locks (small coley). I had a chuckle to myself thinking about the amounts that we had caught on the trawlers and how many hours sleep we had lost for very little money with this type of fish. Just about to go back on board when a local asked me if Andy Jensen had been on board. I later discovered that he was Andy's father. Raymond Evans noticed me talking to him and took him aboard the ship to have a look round and to have a yarn. I took my leave and turned in for the night.

Next morning it had been decided by the Skipper and owners that we would be returning to Hirtshals to put the trawl gear off ready for the Mackerel Season. A few of the crew returned, some with their wives. The rest took personal items off that they had purchased whilst on their shopping trips in Denmark or the UK. Before we sailed Agga took me ashore to show me his home high in the mountains which was a timber framed building and looked very cosy. His wife made me welcome. I also learned that he would be bringing his son Marius as trainee. Some people were saying that he wouldn't hack it being at sea. Years later I learned that Marius was a master of one of Maersk's largest container ships. It just goes to show how people can get things so wrong. I found him very willing to learn and quite a pleasant lad who spoke very good English.

Just after lunch we were leaving Torshavn heading to Hirtshals. All the fish tanks were full, not with fish but water, as we were getting them ready for Mackerel or Herring fishing.

We are now tied up alongside in Hirtshals. It had not been all plain sailing as midway across the Skagerrak and having just passed a few large vessels, the steering decided to pack up. One moment we were on course then the next minute we were turning hard to starboard at **Full Speed**. The engines were put to STOP but then displayed two red lights stating that we were not in command of the ship. Within minutes the secondary steering motor was put on whilst the engineers discovered the fault in the steering which were flat, worn, brushes on the motor causing the problem. Soon we were underway again.

The Grimsby Lady Tied Up in Hirtshals

The next problem we encountered was with the RSW tanks not being emptied fully of water. When we touched the bottom at the entrance to the Harbour, we feared that the main sonar may have sustained damage. This was soon confirmed when it was inspected by a specialist who came aboard to test the system. The inspector sent a diver down to confirm the damage. Meanwhile most of the crew were getting the pelagic trawl off for an overhaul. This was taken into a factory which specialised in this type of work. The very next day we were on a floating dock in Aalborg having repairs to the sonar. The crew's wives started to appear after the crossing all looking GREEN AT THE GILLS. During the evening, using Skagen radio, I had a link call home. It was not like today with the internet and mobiles.

Sailed from Alborg three days after being in the floating dock. The repairs have all been completed. The sonar had a fibre glass cover replaced. We are all up and running and now tied up in Hirtshals. This afternoon we put a spare purse net on board. The net we have is a smaller version of the purse net which is used mainly for sardines. The spare we are putting onboard as a back-up if we damage the main net. The Faroese wives have flown home and we now have the full complement of men onboard. The grocer came on board again with a tray of pastries. Some of the crews are going ashore tonight but I'm not bothering as I am feeling a little apprehensive as I've never done this type of fishing before. I'm sure that I will be ok.

We left Hirtshals just after lunch but not before we had fresh stores put aboard with another full tray of Danish pastries, jam, almond tasting icing sugar, all freshly made. Ropes put away, gangway ladder stored, cook surprised us all with a full English breakfast. Shorer, the cook, asked Raymond Evans what a full English consisted of and once he had made the first one, we had this breakfast almost every Sunday.

On leaving the Harbour a few locals shouted at us wishing us safe sailing and waved us off. As we slowly disappeared from their view and half an hour from leaving port, the water tanks, RSW's, were once more filled to over flowing and then promptly emptied. They were then half filled to give us a little ballast. A few ships, both large and small, tankers, ferries and general cargo were all going about their business. A few smaller fishing boats, fully laden with sand eels were running back to port to discharge their catch. I wasn't on watch until teatime so I decided to have a couple of hours sleep but not before I read a few Danish Gardening Magazines. I wasn't able, at this time, to read the print but the pictures were self-explanatory.

Passing lots of jack up rigs. North Sea pioneers searching for oil in the Scottish waters and gas fields in the Humber area. All these areas which used to be traditional fishing grounds are being taken away. The nets are closing in on the industry, as they say. The issue isn't just the placement areas but pipelines which are like veins crisscrossing the ocean floors.

We will soon be passing Sum Burgh Head, with Fair Isle nearby. We are running at half speed with all three sonars and fish plotters searching for, preferably, mackerel because quotas are being put on the Herring fisheries. I'm now feeling excited and looking forward to a 'new concept' for me as I have not done this type of fishing before. Both Raymond and Garry Evans keep telling me to stop worrying and that I will soon pick up the knowledge of Purse Seining.

Whilst using the sonars and searching for fish marks, the weather suddenly became a full Southerly gale. The wind, prior to this, had been light but we noticed from quite a distance away, squalls with heavy rain, were appearing on the Radar. In no time at all they were upon us and we began dodging to RONA which is a small island off the North Coast of Scotland. We were soon under shelter, close to the land on the Northsides. It was decided to drop the Anchor and wait the storm out. Whist on anchor watch, mid-afternoon, we could see sheep and goats climbing down the mountains to lower ground to feed. Apparently, a Scottish farmer had the rights for keeping these animals on the island. No sooner had the gale hit us than it went away just as quickly. The anchor was then lifted and we were slowly in search of fish once more.

After 18 hours at anchor, the weather had dropped away considerably. The decision was made to leave Loch Eribol to resume searching for fish. A few other vessels had come into the Loch to shelter from the winds. On the bridge, as we were lifting the anchor, the Faroese Skipper put the sonars on sweeping the sea areas. As we were coming up to an island before leaving the Loch, the Skipper became excited on hearing a different tone coming from the Wesmar Sonar. Quite near the island we started to turn to starboard, at slow speed, looking to see how large the shoal could be.

The sun had just set, with us still turning to starboard and we were told to standby to cast the net. With all crew standing by, another boat, a certain Scottish purser, tried to cut inside. As quick as a flash, when the boat came out of our heading, the sound of 'CLARY', could be heard coming from the bridge. This shout indicated that I should take up my position with a Faroese crew member, Gutty, who was the Skippers brother, standing on top of the purse net. The ship was now in total darkness apart from its navigation lights.

A loud SHOUT came from the Bridge, 'BOUYAN OUT!' The tail end of the net was thrown over from the net bin which had weights and worked like a small parachute filling with water. This in turn pilled the rest of the net. With the sound of clang, clang, clang, the bottom part of the net and the floats came out in unison. From the safety of the walkway two yellow lights were flashing from the 'Monkey Island' (the name for the bridge top).

With my job done I soon grabbed a large coffee and a couple of smokes. The net we were using was 1,500 meters by 150 metres deep. The net had been used usually for catching Sardines. The Skipper of the Scottish purser kept shining his searchlights into our net areas before we could close the net but this failed to have any impact. He shot his net soon after and lost half his net!

After having a quick smoke and a strong coffee, Gutty and I returned to the after deck. The forward team had heaved on the purse wires which in turn closed the net. The net was then fed into the triple block and the single block hung above the net bin. When the linkages came near the triple block it was released from the wire cable which went through both types of blocks. As the net started to go into the net bin the wire and clip link was attached to a steel bar and wire. Once more the rest of the net had to be separated. Weights were on the inside net, in the middle were the floats, on the top, up to six people were in the net bin, flaking the net, laying down the floats and attaching the clips. During this operation the net had picked up huge amounts of Jellyfish which rained down on us, stinging our face, hands and any bare skin which was painful. We soon became accustomed to this happening and protected ourselves by putting Vaseline on our face's and bare skin.

Slowly but surely the net came in. I had been called to the fish separator and my job now was to divert the fish into separate tanks keeping the ships stability level. With the purse net tight alongside the ships side the suction pump was then put into the fish which [together with sea water] were pumped in to the tanks on board.

After a few hours pumping and with a decent haul of 500 ton of large mackerel we made our way slowly into the

Minch to unload the catch to the Klondike's near the westside port of Ullapool.

After pumping the haul of mackerel onboard we are now outside Ullapool Harbour were there are a number of Klondike's which are what we call factory vessels, all from the eastern bloc. They are all awaiting the purse seiners to discharge catches of Mackerel. There are already a number of boats tied alongside discharging. We have been given orders to go alongside the designated factory vessel. We are tied up on the ships starboard side which has a large black fender keeping us both from doing any damage. Our mate, using a large pole, measures how much fish is in each tank.

The Net Weights

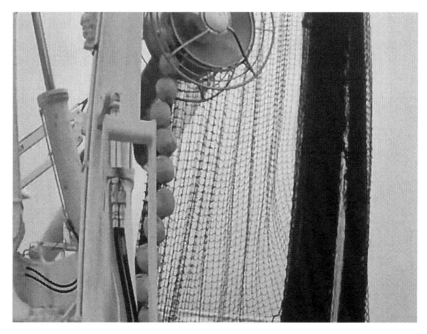

Net Being Returned to the Net Bin

Net Ready for Casting

Tanks of Fish Being Closed

Our fish is then transferred and weighed in to large tanks, either by pumping into tanks or loading by net bailing. We unloaded 200 ton to one ship and a further 300 ton to another vessel. After finishing pumping fish, we left the area to continuing searching for Mackerel. The tanks have been washed out ready for the next fish. After a successful evening it was now time to have a nap whilst we are able.

There have been a few reports of large shoals just North of Rona. Just a few days ago we had been laid under the land because of the weather. We are about ten miles north west of the island with ten or so purse seiners all searching for mackerel. Mid-afternoon our sonars started to give us a good indication that we had hit a mark (shoal). Now the ship started to plot the fish's movements. It was around teatime and the sun was setting once more.

Having had a few hours' sleep and feeling refreshed all hands were sent for an early tea. A few boats were close by doing basically the same as us. With tea finished the order of 'CLARY' could be heard once more and 'BOUYAN OUT!' soon followed. With the end thrown over and within a few moments we had started to retrieve the net. The weather had been kind with a light breeze and a little rain.

Soon we were in the net bin flaking the net. The moonlight was shining on the sea, casting off a sparkling glow. Soon after we stopped folding the net, floats, etc. and I took up my position at the Fish Separator. Lifting one door then another whilst the fish pump kept pumping and pumping. Within a space of time, we had filled six tanks with large Mackerel. The time was now coming up to midnight and the decision had been made to cast the net again. With that haul we managed to fill the remaining tanks catching a similar number of fish. With the tanks more or less full and with plenty of mackerel left in the net, we let go of the end which released the fish to swim away.

With two or three hours getting back to Ullapool, Raymond Evans, the English Skipper and a Faroese watch mate did the watch whilst the rest of us grabbed an hour or so before landing the fish. Just before 1300 hours we were called to go alongside the Young World which was a large fishing vessel in itself, and like the rest of the Klondyker's, was unable to fish in UK waters. I seem to remember that this ship we were unloading to, had been either the Grand Banks or Labrador and that she had been in a collision. The size of the hole, following the collision was the size of a double decker bus. Now we are tied up alongside with three of our nine hatches open.

Purse Seine

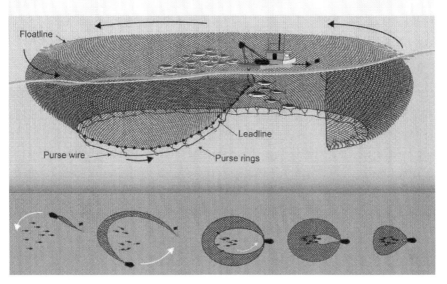

We started brailling the fish out of the tanks. The Braille net consisted of a metal frame with a large, heavy bar, built on the front with a large net shaped in the same way as the nets we used on the beach or in a pond. This net had to be dipped into the tank which then filled with Mackerel. When filled the net held almost five tons in weight. Attached to the bottom of the net a quick release clip was fitted which when pulled releases the fish into the Klondyker's tanks.

It had been my job to ensure that when the braille went into the hold it was lowered into the tanks at an angle. The fish was taken out using our forward crane which went on to the vessel. Working at three-hour intervals, followed by a break of say 30 minutes, we were discharging until just after midnight. A few of the crew on the Klondyker's peered over their ships rail and they all looked similar to Boris Yeltsin, small, stocky and powerfully built. A few women also looked curiously over the rail at our ship. I don't think that I would have liked to argue with them either, as they were built in a similar way to the men. Conditions on the ship must have been dire, as the smell coming from the ship made me feel dirty.

We were lucky, I suppose, as we had better conditions. We had a nice clean ship which we all took our turn cleaning and washing down weekly. Just after 0200 hours we had finished with the landing brailler, put away hatches, secured followed by the exchange of the paperwork. We eventually let go of the ropes and headed alongside to Ullapool harbour with a small job to do down the Engine room and new hydraulic pump coming from Aberdeen. We were soon tied up alongside. The harbour gangway ladder deployed and I had a quick shower which I felt that I needed. Garry Evans volunteered to take the watch in harbour until breakfast time. That is one thing that I've learnt over the years 'NEVER VOLUNTEER!

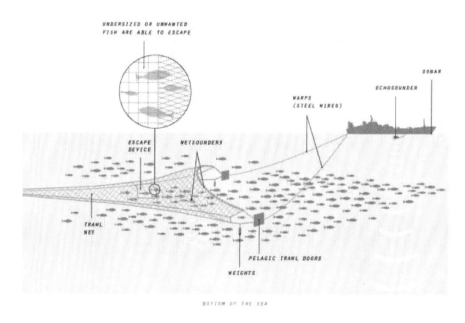

Pelagic Nets Used for Catching Blue Whiting

After tying up alongside in Ullapool all hands went for breakfast. Large bowl of eggs, toast or cereals washed down with a nice cuppa. We are only waiting for our new fish pump to arrive which should be with us mid-morning. I decided to go ashore and stretch my legs and I was told not to be too long, as we will be sailing as soon as the part comes.

I think from the quay we had to walk up a slight hill where there were a few shops and a couple of pubs but it had been too early to grab a pint. I found a paper shop/off-licence and picked up a couple of papers with possibly a Scottish Gardening Magazine. A couple of the Faroese lads came ashore buying odds and ends for their needs. A few crews from the Klondyker's had been ashore asking for Vodka. That's a drink I have never ever liked. There had been a story circulating around that an Eastern Bloc ship had brought all the tins of Cat food believing that it had actually been 'cat meat' in the tins. How disappointing for them!

As we came out of the shop a lorry with our new pump was passing us. Good timing! We made our way down the hill and reached the ship as the pump was being lifted on to our ship. We went up the gangway ladder and gave a hand to let go. I was informed that I am on watch after lunch, so now time to grab an hour or two sleep.

Just before lunch I was called out for the afternoon watch. I was sitting on my seat locker with a strong coffee that the watch had brought to me, with the usual fag in hand. I had a quick wash to get the sleep out of my eyes, brushed my teeth and took a leisurely stroll to the messdeck. Most of the crew had been there feeding their faces. I'm sitting mainly with the Faroese crew and sampling their food. The cook, on occasions, did both English meals with Faroese/Danish meals. I filled my coffee cup and had a chip butty with Daddies sauce. It's the comfort food that we have at home, even today.

Now I've taken over the watch heading towards an area North West of Rona to a position where we had caught the two large hauls. Gutty, the skipper's brother is on watch with me and he knows more about the sonar and the sounds it makes when we find any shoals. Don't get me wrong, it's a learning process and I am gaining experience daily. On a Northerly heading at slow speed, both Wesmar Sonars sweeping the sea bed, every 15 minutes plotting our course. The fish finder running in the back ground, everything in our favour.

Midway through the afternoon watch when, just astern of us, came the Fishery Protection Vessel, HMS Guernsey requesting to board our ship for an inspection. I sent my watchmate down to call Raymond Evans so that that he could give permission for them to board the vessel. Ray had been up all morning doing the paperwork for the landings via Klondyker's. He soon appeared on the Bridge. I told him what was what and all he said he was; 'I could do without this!' Within twenty minutes, a team of Sailors were onboard going about their business which was to check the ships log and the areas where we have caught the fish. Agga, the Faroese Skipper, took over my watch whilst I took a couple of sailors around the ship looking at our purse net stored in the bin which had contained mackerel from the last haul.

Next, they looked into the raw tanks which were empty. They then went to the fore hold where they checked the nets, mesh sizes etc. They were soon back onto the bridge where the full crew were assembled [looking bewildered] whilst the naval officer checked each individual's paperwork and passport. One of the lads asked; 'Are we criminals?'

With the reply asking; 'ARE YOU?' Within an hour or so of the inflatable coming alongside, they were going back onboard their own ship. There must have been about twenty vessels in our area and we were the only one that they had boarded and this wasn't to be the ONLY time.

After these events I took over the watch and Ray went back to bed. I was feeling sorry for Ray, having to deal with the Protection Boat and its visit but he just shrugged it off. Talking to Agga with a lot general chit chat when he suddenly turned around to the sonars. He had detected a sound known only to him from experience. Rubbing his hands and smiling to me saying we have a good mark of fish.

On the sounder, the mark we had found looked like a big polo mint. A blue circle with a deep red inner circle. With the sun setting and just before tea, I was told to call the crew out but to leave Ray in. Fifteen minutes later everyone took their position and 'CLARY' was called and soon after, the call 'BUOYAN OUT'. I threw the tail-end over, quickly scrambling off the net to safety. The weights were going out with the steel rings and floats all going over in unison. With the men in position, we were all ready for the next procedure of closing the net with the metal ring clips and cable wires. Soon the net was in the top block and threaded through the triplex block. Most of the crew relieved each other to get our tea.

Working in total darkness, except for the fixed red and yellow flashing lights, together with the navigation lights. Occasionally our search light would shine towards our net directing the fish. Apparently, as we began to flake the net into the net bin, large silver scales started to appear.

WHAT COULD IT BE?????

After the events with the Fishery Protection this afternoon, we had shot our net away within hours of them departing our area. With the net being in the top block and triple block we started to retrieve our net. Most of the crew have had their tea. I almost forgot to apply a light film of Vaseline on my face. We are now seeing plenty of jelly fish and the occasional Portuguese Man of War which are large purple coloured jelly fish with long tentacles. We are also seeing plenty of fish scales shining like confetti as the night sky shines above. On two occasions I had stopped the hauling, as we had a couple of 'granddad' dover soles in the net. I had never caught them before near the Minch and I was thinking; 'That will do nicely for supper!'

When we had pulled nearly all the slack net in, we made our way to different areas to receive the fish. Looking over the starboard side I could see the mouth of the net open, with large yellow floats. The fish were trying to escape over the top but with the mate working the triple block, this prevented any more fish escaping. Slowly the pump was lowered into the water and we started the hydraulic pump which began to suck the fish out of the net.

We had caught a LARGE haul of HERRING and as we started pumping away the sea sparkled a lot more with the herring scales. I had been in charge of the fish tank and chutes, with the help from the skipper, trying to keep the tanks even as we pumped away. We had filled three of our seven tanks when I was told to go aft and chill whilst the ship looked for another mark.

It did not take long to find and within two hours we had filled another three tanks but this time with mackerel. By 0100 hours we had finished. All the tanks secured and we were bound to a secret destination to discharge our catch.

Raymond Evans took the first watch and I would be going on watch after breakfast. As I was leaving the deck I had been thinking; 'If this had been cod and haddock how long would it have taken to gut them all!'

Its nearly forty hours since we started steaming and we have reached our destination. We sailed up a small fjord and alongside the quay under the cover of darkness where we immediately started to discharge our catch of fish. We were unloading straight in to open back lorries which took the fish straight into the factory for processing. We had been invited into the factory after unloading and became amazed how smoothly the factory ran, with conveyor belts, filleting machines, sized and sorted into freezers, then packed into cartons. Amazing!

Just before breakfast we were underway again and heading back to the fishing grounds. The RSW water tanks were filled until they overflowed. All the main decks were washed down with the fire hoses making sure we had left no tell-tale signs of catching Herring. We had landed 350 ton of herring and 400 tons of large mackerel. Not bad for a night's work.

When we arrived back at the fishing grounds a couple of ships asked whether we had been in for a landing. The answer had been NO! We had been in with a small problem with a hydraulic pipe. This was only a small white lie. We went straight on to the grounds and we found another large mark. A certain ship tried bully tactics to try and makes us move on but knowing our skipper this wouldn't be happening. Just after 2200 hours the cry came 'BUOYAN OUT!'

Clang, clang, clang, had been the noise made by the rings on the net as it passed over the side. You had to be quick on your feet standing on top of the purse net and throwing the tail end over the side in pitch dark. I had it off to a fine art, holding the net on the rail when the order was given, letting go as I'm leaving the area and retreating to the safety of the walk way.

I then had time for a quick smoke before going into the bin area. This haul, as usual, has gone smoothly. Flaking the net, folding the floats, all preparations so it would go out again smoothly. However, this haul had been no good to us as the mackerel sizes proved to be all juvenile fish which went back in the sea. A waste of time and effort for us but luckily this type of fishing means that although we can catch a few tons each time, we can release fish back into the sea without killing any. This is different to trawling where the net is pulled behind the ship and the fish literally drown.

We have now recovered the net and in position for when needed. We are just a couple of miles outside the Minch close to Cape Wrath. Most of the lads have had a bite to eat with the last of the deck crew coming inside for a brew. We were just about to pour a coffee when over the Tannoid 'CLARY!' was the message which was a warning for us to 'STANDBY!' I managed to take my coffee on the deck where I was standing at my Post. Nearly forty minutes later the call to throw the end over (BUOYAN OUT) came from the bridge.

We have cast the purse once more but little did we know that during this haul, after we had put the net back over, we were just sitting outside the entrance to the accommodation, when the fire alarm had been set off. Putting my cigarette out I walked to our muster station, quickly putting a lifejacket over my head, securing the straps around my waist, and waited for information. Musters are an important part of running a safe environment. We all had a purposeful position to complete to ensure the safety of the ship and crew. Having a head count is the most important task of the skipper/mate duties. We are then sent to complete important tasks such as closing vents, closing water tight doors, wearing warm clothing is always drilled in to us. After maybe fifteen minutes we were all told to stand down. Apparently, an engineer had spilled oil on an exhaust pipe causing the fire alarm to be activated. I was making my way to the mess for a quick coffee and a strange smell was in the air. I can only describe the smell as being similar to cat's pee. This smell was very quickly followed by my eyes smarting and others started to have the same problem. Opening the doors and turning the extractors back on soon cleared the AREAS.

I am now taking up my position in the net bin and we started to flake the net again. I had forgotten to put any Vaseline on my face and my skin soon started to burn and itch. Twenty minutes later I rinsed my face in the changing room and the 2nd engineer passed me a coffee. I began to feel the relief straight away and applied a little Vaseline to my face. A bit late, as they say, 'shutting the stable door after the horse has bolted!' came to mind.

With the purse closed too we began pumping large mackerel, weighing three to a kilo. Opening this chute, then the next being the after tanks, soon these were also full. Now we are filling the centre tanks.

I had been relieved now and am having a warm drink and maybe a sarnie or soup. Although it's about June or July it can still get cold at night. After about twenty minutes I returned to the fish chutes, where the middle tanks were nearly full as well. The Faroese Mate came along with a large pole which he dipped into the tanks saying only five more minutes before they are full and then use the forward tanks. You could feel the ship begin to wallow a bit, as we are now putting extra fish into the fore tanks. Sea Water is now running across the decks.

We have been pumping nearly five hours when the Skipper shouted in Faroese to the Mate. I looked towards the Bridge when Agga, the Skipper told me that we were going to HIRTSHALS when we have finished pumping. By Midnight we were underway. I was told that I would be taking the first steaming watch. Just after 0200 hours we were underway and the Skipper says to me the I'm his lucky mascot. We have caught over 600 ton tonight. With a bad forecast and a good price to be made for our fish, it was SMILES all-round as we slid slowly through the waves, as we have just past Cape Wrath.

This time tomorrow afternoon we should be alongside in Hirtshals. We will be landing as soon as we arrive or so I've been informed. I have just come off watch at breakfast time when I handed over the watch to Raymond, showing him our last position on the chart. I signed off the radio and the watch log. I went into the messdeck and began enjoying a Full English minus the Black pudding. I soon consumed what was put in front of me as I was feeling hungry as the smell of fresh bread had reached us on the bridge.

One or two of the lads were watching both televisions at once. We had two sets placed one above the other but the sound was only being played on one set, the Danish television. They used to show plenty of Laurel and Hardie films and the Faroese used to be in stitches watching them. I duly finished my meal and rinsed my plate whilst approaching the dishwasher. From the corner of my eye, I saw a large bowl containing sheep's heads. I did a double take to make sure I was not seeing things. Shorer, the Faroese Cook, couldn't stop laughing at the look on my face. He then said; 'Don't worry, they're not for you. You're having a mixed grill.' I told him; 'I might take my meal to my Cabin at tea time!'

I then ventured out onto the foredeck to get some fresh air and I had been peering inside one of the holding tank inspection hatches when I noticed that there were a few haddock, cod, coley, ling, etc which were floating on the surface. The Faroese Skipper saw me looking at the fish and I asked if I could have some for-stocker money. Although he didn't understand what I meant he still said yes. I used a couple of red baskets with handles and I began gutting the fish, throwing the entrails, livers etc over the side of the ship. We soon had a following of Herring Gulls waiting for the titbits.

One of the Faroese deckhands, called Finnur, came and gave me a hand. I soon had five or six full baskets, all sorted, washed and cleaned. I went to the cook and asked if I could put them in the chiller and I will either sell them or give them away. Little did I know that the first person I asked if they were interested in the fish, took all that I had and paid me in kroners. Me being me, I bought a couple of rounds in the Skiperkrone but that's another story. Having cleaned the fish and washed the deck area I decided to have a sauna but I did not intend to use the COLD SHOWER, this time!

In the early hours, with six or so more hours to go before we dock, it had been a nightmare. The amount of Traffic (boats) that we passed and altered our course for was unbelievable and I think I have said before, that the number of ships entering and leaving the Skagerrak and moving in all directions of the compass was incredible. Sometimes I felt as though I had my head between my arse, as it were. When Ray relieved me at 0300 hours the shipping had become lighter.

I was awoken by the sound of the thrusters just after 1000 hours. My cabin had been directly above the motor and as we were about to enter the harbour, we felt a slight bump. The ship then went into stern gear, as we slowly came away from the harbour. The last time we hit the bottom it had cost a lot of money to have the sonar fixed but it had been decided to take some water out of the RSW. This in turn lightened the ship and in a short period of time we entered the Harbour without incident ready for docking.

Just before lunch we started to unload. Marks & Spencer's Quality Control came onboard taking numerous samples from the six tanks. Earlier, we had received the go ahead to land the Mackerel and my first job was to tip the bailer into the tank which then went into a large open lorry. This was taken to the factory, returning to be reloaded and three lorries were used for this operation. Landing crews were relieving each other with smoke breaks etc.

My next job was to climb in the lorry which, no doubt, Health and Safety would not allow this today. When the bailer landed on to the wagon my task was to keep the fish level. Alongside the wagons were women and children picking any overspilled fish that landed on the ground, which they put into baskets and buckets and were sold on to fish merchants or for their own use. I kept sweeping a few over the side, just to give a little help, shall we say.

Climbing off the lorry, I ventured into the fish market and seeing someone with overalls I approached him and told him that I had some other fish to sell. We had just a little problem with the language barrier but an agreement was soon reached. I took the fish from the chiller and on to the quayside. It took little time but a few of the crew helped me to drag the red baskets ashore. The fish were then tipped into boxes and our baskets were put back on board our ship. The transaction complete I took my position back in the lorry once more. As I climbed off the lorry the fish merchant gave me an envelope stuffed with money. With a fistful of kroners, it felt like happy days. By teatime we had finished landing. After our meal had been served the Faroese mate Sverry came into the mess giving all hands their share of the landing money. As I held my hand out for my share, with a wink of his eye, telling me that I didn't need the money, as I had my own landing arrangement.

After landing I had my tea and grabbed an hour on the seat locker in my cabin. Most of the crew were going ashore. I had been invited along with Ray and Gary but they were not coming. Just before 2000 hours I took my turn in the shower in preparation for going ashore for a few beers with the crew in the Skiperkrone (local pub). I think that I had a link call home to let Cheryl know that we had landed and were down for sailing after lunchtime tomorrow. I also let her know that I would be going out with the crew and her reply was not to overdo it! By 2100 hours I was sitting at the bar having a pilsner. By 2200 hours we were drinking Carlsberg Elephant beer and it was going down so smoothly, just like amber nectar.

A few crews were in from the purser fleet. A ships bell hung over the bar and each time it rang, the person who rang the bell would buy everyone in the bar a drink. I went to sit at the other end of the bar to make sure I did not ring it. The music seemed to get louder, as did the people who drunkenly tried to talk. Without breaking any confidence there were one or two of our crew who had the local girls in hand. As the night drew on and still necking a few beers, but I didn't take the option of drinking Shorts or Snaps. I'm glad I didn't as I barely remember leaving the establishment and getting back to the ship.

Mid-morning, am I dreaming. I'm sure I can hear someone calling me. I opened my eyes and saw daylight. I swiftly closed them again. I heard a voice saying that we were getting our pelagic trawl back soon. I managed to crawl out of my bunk. I reached the bathroom with an eruption of vomit coming out of my mouth. I just managed to open the toilet door and emptied my stomach contents in the bowl. I seemed to lay with my head on the bottom of the porcelain toilet. One of the crew asked if I was alright. I think I groaned my reply.

Eventually I picked myself up, had a shower with the water nearly scalding me. Soon I was entering the messdeck and put two eggs in a glass with a drop of milk and swiftly drank it. This soon settled my stomach together with a couple of painkillers. I felt absolutely terrible but the crew went ashore and were acting as though they had not even had a drink.

I was summoned to the bridge to use the Hydraulic Net Drum to recover our net, as we were tied up with the stern to the quay, alongside the net repairers. We attached the ends, heaving slowly and we soon had our net coiled on the drum, putting a tarpaulin cover over the net. Lunch time soon passed and by 1400 hours we were heading out to sea again in search of a decent catch.

We had sailed through the Minch, passed through the Kyle of LoCash and I didn't realise how narrow the channels had been. We are hunting for mackerel but without any success. The orders from our agent telling us that we should look for blue whiting.

We are now heading towards Belfast to get things sorted as we have a problem with a generator. Never in all my years of going to sea have I seen the size of the buoyage system, they seemed massive. After tying up the ropes we were alongside Gallagher's Cigarette factory. We soon obtained clearance from the Customs and Immigration and we were allowed ashore. After leaving the dock areas we came across large tents where security checked that we were not carrying any weapons. I am glad I had my passport with me as this meant I was soon cleared by the officials. One of the Officers pulled me to one side telling me that I would be perfectly safe as long as I didn't speak about Religion or Politics.

I found a little pub and walked in but straight away felt uneasy. Just behind the bar were bullet holes from when the pub had a visit! A local approached me and asked who I was and what was I doing there. Once I told him that I was a fisherman and the group I was with were Faroese I was made welcome. On this occasion I really did have just one pint then swiftly left the pub. I picked up a few things, I think maybe from Woolworth's and we then made our way back to the ship not before being searched again.

Within half an hour the repair was sorted and we sailed. I remember Raymond Evans saying to me that I had been braver than him as he wouldn't have gone into town. It wasn't the case of being braver and looking back, I now realise it was probably a stupid idea.

Only alongside Belfast for six hours and we have set sail again. The large lettering of Harland and Wolffe were slowly getting smaller as we neared the entrance of the Irish Sea. I had been on the ships wheel hand steering until we came out of the roads and auto was now working which made lighter work for navigating.

We had sailed just before teatime and now I have been relieved by the Faroese Mate and we have set a course line where reports of decent catches of blue whiting are being caught. We should be there before breakfast, all being well. For tea we are having ham, eggs and chips as the Faroese were having rass fish which smelt rotten with a vile smelling sauce. I was offered a taste which I politely refused, with roars of laughter coming from there table.

I have started to pick up various bits of the Faroese language, mainly swear words to be honest, but it's a start. Tea time had finished and I watched the news on the telly then rolled in for the night. I had been in a deep sleep and I have now been called out in preparation to put the net in the water but not before I had a couple of smokes along with a pot of tea. I was soon fully alert and on hoping on to the deck the weather had freshened to a force six.

The net rolled off the net drum without any hook ups. The float lines came up which we held until we placed the transducer in to its pocket of net and attached. the clevis cable which indicated how much fish would be in the net. The doors are now being lowered as we are back pelagic fishing once again.

Four hours into the fishing operations and we started to decompress the fish by hauling 50 fathoms, in intervals. If the net came up too quickly, we could split the net which we had previously done on just one occasion. At that time the cod ends, came to the surface, similar to a whale leaping out of the water. The result was that the cod ends erupted all the fish to the surface.

We were informed on the deck speakers to be careful as the weather was now a force 8. We are being thrown about a bit as we are Hauling with the wind being on the stern with a few corkscrews thrown in to make things easier. There is not much room to stand on the after deck, perhaps thirty feet, with six people working. Soon the starboard door came up without any problems and it was made secure by chain. The pennant had been unhooked from its 'G' link. The port door came up at an angle which had been lowered then heaved on again but it still came up at the wrong angle. Without mentioning any names, the person I had been working with suddenly approached the pennant clips and the door suddenly swung into its holding position but not before hitting the unnamed person, who thankfully was wearing a hard hat.

I shouted out to the other deck crew that we had an injured person. The decision, after the injured man was given a primary survey, was made to take the man inside the ship in the changing room area out of the bad weather. Ray Evans contacted the medical services ashore who made the decision to airlift him to the hospital. I was given a radio where I listened on channel 72 which was a rescue channel used on VHF.

Whilst awaiting medical assistance we reassured the injured person, in both English and Faroese, that he would soon in safe hands. We were all very concerned as he had blood coming out of one of his ears. We didn't remove his hard hat, we kept him calm, warm and dry.

A Changing Room Similar to those on 'Grimsby Lady'

Within half hour or so I could hear static on the ships radio then Ray's voice asking if I had copied that. I replied that I had not heard the message. He came off the bridge to tell us that the Helicopter flight 501 was on its way. I will always remember this number as I had a pair of Levi jeans with the same number.

The Helicopter soon reached our position. We had been informed to take the injured person on to the foredeck for transportation and that they would be using their own stretcher. The Helicopter was soon overhead and when they were just over the bridge area when slowly a man came down a high wire. We were instructed not to touch the rope when he was being lowered down. I repeated the command but with the language barrier one of our crew didn't heed the advice, grabbing the tail end of the rope. As he reached out to grab the line, the only way I can describe what happened was a bright flash of light, followed by a crackling sound, followed by a loud piercing scream which echoed in the night air. The crew member made his way off the foredeck seeking treatment for the burns on his hands.

The transfer of the crew member with the head injury was quite easy. I had a quick chat with the medic who said that he couldn't do our job and I replied that I couldn't do his either. We soon had the injured man in the helicopter. I held the guideline from the stretcher then with a signal telling me to let go off the line, we were soon sitting in the MESSDECK recalling the nights events. A message came from the bridge stating that we would be shooting the nets again shortly.

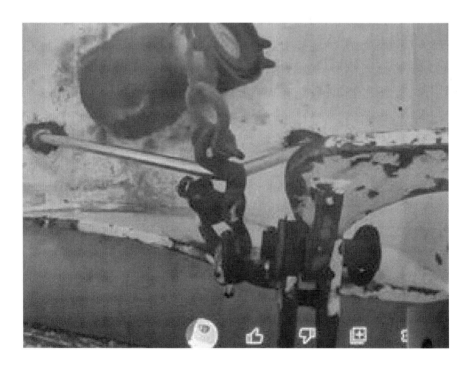

Trawl Doors and Pennant Clips

After a couple of days, we had a message saying that the injured person had been sent home suffering from a mild concussion. Following this incident, when working on deck, we all started wearing our hard hats!

We docked in Plymouth and the owner; Fred Parkes came to visit the ship. He asked me how long I had been at sea and did I want Cheryl to join the ship next time that we docked in Denmark, all expenses paid. I telephoned Cheryl to find out her thoughts and to my surprise she said YES. Of course, this was after talking to her mum, as she would be watching the children.

A short time later we had docked in Hirtshals but we wouldn't be landing our catch until the morning, I now had to be on my best behaviour as Cheryl would be joining us tonight or early morning. Just after teatime I set off from Hirtshals going to Aalborg Airport. I arrived about 2130 hours and the flight was due to arrive at around 2200 hours. I made my way to the bar, ordered a beer or two as I waited for the announcement of the plane's arrival. I had just had a couple of pints when Cheryl came into the airport lounge. I had been talking to a man who was going home and he was travelling the same way as us. He suggested that we could share the cost of our taxi and I agreed. Soon we were on our travels. We were asked if we would like stop at his house and have a nightcap and then travel onwards to our destination. I always found the Danes extremely friendly and hospitable.

Just after midnight we were climbing up the gangway ladder. I put Cheryl's case in my cabin, had a mug of tea and then rolled in for the night, I think that Cheryl had done very well, as she had never flown before. She flew, Humberside to Amsterdam, Amsterdam to Copenhagen, Copenhagen to Aalborg.

After collecting the wife from the airport, we eventually joined the ship in Hirtshals. I remember Ray and Gary saying to Cheryl that they hoped she would not be sea sick. Her reply was, 'What, with my heritage!' She meant that her father, grandfather and great grandfather were all trawler skippers and that fishing had been in her blood. I think she would have been less confident if she knew the weather we were about to experience.

The next morning, we were discharging the catch of mackerel on to lorries destined for Marks and Spencer's distributors. Soon the time came for us to sail and on leaving the safety of the harbour the weather began to freshen. The first sign of bad weather was the lifting of the ships head as it met the oncoming seas. Then the rising of the stern and once or twice the propellor seemed to leave the water, sending a judder through the ship. To me this was not a problem and felt like nothing at all as I was used to these movements. However, for Cheryl, who had never been to sea before, it must have been a very scary time. She soon became seasick and I fetched a bucket for her to save her having to run to and from the toilet area. After a few hours I had to leave the cabin to take my watch. On returning I brought some cream crackers and fizzy orange, so that she would have something to bring up, instead of just bile.

The weather abated slightly and I suggested that we should go on the bridge to get some fresh air and to see the horizon which may help with her sickness. When we reached the bridge level the ship was dipping into a huge wave and all she saw was the horizon plummeting in front of our eyes.

We went down three flights of stairs very quickly, as there was a toilet at the bottom of the stairs and we soon returned to our cabin. I tried to help her by suggesting that she kept her shoulder against the bulkhead which would help with her balance and steady her motion whilst walking along the alleyways. That didn't work out so well, as the first thing she did was to bump into a fire extinguisher which was hung against the bulk head. I was not the flavour of the month and she accused me of trying to kill her, so that I could claim the insurance money!

Who me? Would I do such a thing to my lovely wife!

After a couple of days, when the bad weather eased and she started to get over the sea sickness (although she was still a very strange colour), she ventured towards the messdeck, walking through the galley space. John, the cook, asked her how she was and could she manage something to eat. She asked if she could have some toast and a pot of tea. It was at this point that she spotted some sheep's heads being defrosted in one of the galley sinks! The smell of the very strong coffee and the cigarette smoke made her turn pale but she soon got over it. When I walked into the Messdeck Cheryl had been sitting with John the cook. I joined the company and as the rest of the crew came in, I introduced Cheryl to the Faroese crew. Raymond Evans and his brother Garry sat with us.

In the messdeck most of our crew were having breakfast and we sat down with Ray and Garry. Agga, the fishing skipper, told Cheryl that she should have some eggs with her toast, telling her that 'they are very good for the bollocks!' She answered him by saying 'it's not me who has the bollocks but men!' Laughter rang out in the messdeck.

We have been laid most of the day and now that the daylight is slowly disappearing this is when the mackerel begin to rise from the seabed, especially if there is a full moon. We had been keeping an eye on a decent mark and just before 2000 hours we were called to the sound once more of 'CLARY' (meaning standby). Once again, I took up my position on top of the net bin, holding the end of the purse net which, when thrown overboard, enabled the rest of the net to pullout into the water. After what seemed like an age 'BUOYAN OUT' was shouted which was the signal for me to throw the end over. I then swiftly moved away from the area. Clang-clang-clang went the weights as they hit the side of the ship.

The Purse Net

Photograph Showing Mackerel in Purse Net
(Not Grimsby Lady)

The Weight Clips

With a quick smoke in one hand and a mug of black coffee in the other I slowly took up my position as net folder in the net bin, along with another four or five men. Gutti had been folding the floats whilst Ray, Pete, Garry and me were folding the net and Jormon released the clips. Everything was going smoothly when one of the rings became stuck. These weights were very heavy and were quickly backing up. No one appeared to be able to move them and it seemed to take ages for Sverry, the Mate, to see what was happening. He swiftly came into the bin area and grabbing hold of the ring which released without a problem, with about eight weights pinging along the wire. He gave me a wry smile, more or less saying 'this is how it's done!' He was such a lovely man and I would say 'a gentle giant'. I met his father a few years ago when we had run ashore in what the skipper thought had been straight fjord which turned out not to be, but that's another story.

I climbed out of the net bin, moving to my next job where I was in charge of the washer chutes. I was directing the fish which in this case was mackerel, into one of seven RSW tanks.

I noticed that Cheryl had been standing at the ships rail looking at the mackerel as we attached the fish pump, saying there were fish jumping over the floats. A few did escape but most were pumped aboard. We had been pumping quite a while when the purse became empty and the Mate came towards me with a large pole with a hooped net at the end. He quickly put the pole end into each tank as he had been taking soundings and we had 500 ton on board.

We then went alongside an Eastern Bloc factory ship to unload our catch. We unloaded about half of what we had and moved to another vessel until we were empty. We had landed 510 ton which was not a bad guess using a pole. It just goes to shows that experience does count.

Ray and Garry took the night watch and we dropped anchor close to the entrance to Ullapool. Throughout the trip we fished during the night and did many trips into Ullapool where we discharged our catch. The sea around where we were fishing was so clear it seemed as though you could touch the fish with your hands. As the fish was caught and the tanks were filled, making us heavier, we could see fish swimming by, from the port hole in my cabin.

We had just passed Scrabster heading towards the Minch. The weather had not been the kindest so far but very soon we were in Loch Eribol with our anchor down. We were just doing the anchor watches with the rest of the crew catching up on sleep. Little did we know that on leaving the safety of Loch Eribol we would shoot the purse net and catch nearly 600 tons of large mackerel. We then discharged our catch just outside Ullapool. We gave 300 ton each to Eastern Bloc factory trawlers. These ships had women on board but not like the women we were accustomed to seeing. These were built like all-in-wrestlers, built like brick shit houses.

Soon we had discharged the catch and we then went in search for more. I think that Cheryl has brought us some good luck and seemed to have settled in ok. At first, she was shy with the crew, including the Faroese but that soon passed. She helped John in the galley, to pass away the hours. I enjoyed her company and letting her see how we earned our money catching fish and the skill involved. Agga liked her company on the bridge whilst searching for fish and she made sure to keep out of the way when we were shooting the purse, as there is some dangerous equipment involved in the process. I enjoyed working on this ship with the Faroese, who, like our crew, were related through birth or marriage, in one way or another.

The nest night we cast our net and caught a large shoal of mackerel. Most of the ship that evening had caught plenty of fish which stopped us from discharging to the ship. The decision was made to head to Hirtshals to unload the catch. After breakfast we started to discharge the fish holds. We had an estimate 800 tons of mackerel. We took it in turns with me working the brailler, dipping into the tank, then swinging outboard onto lorries with large trailers. We worked until mid-morning when we had a coffee break.

We had a quick coffee break and we all to return to landing the fish. My job had been to climb in to the back of the lorry to spread the load of fish equally. I noticed there were a couple of youngsters who were eagerly waiting for any spillages which fell from the lorry. They quickly put the fish into a bucket which were then sold to a fish. I kept tipping a few towards them and when I did, they beamed with radiant smiles towards me. I noticed that Cheryl had been watching me and smiled at what I was doing.

Dinnertime soon approached with Cheryl noticing that lying in the galley sink were sheep's heads defrosting for the Faroese evening meal. Just before teatime all the fish holds had been emptied. I think we had a mixed grill for tea whilst the Faroese tucked in to Sheep's heads.

After our meal we soon vacated the mess, had a shower and dressed in some decent clothes to go ashore. We were looking forward to having a goodnight out in the Skiperkrone which was a local pub and disco.

When we reached the watering hole there were a few dancing girls who had been sitting with our crew. When I walked in, I introduced Cheryl by saying 'This is my wife!' I remembering at that time a 'catchy song' that I really liked called 'Son of Jamaica' and I think that Boney M had also covered the same song.

We were all having a good time and at certain times someone would enter the pub and would ring the ships bell which meant that they were buying EVERYONE a drink. I always made sure I kept well away from that bell and although it was tempting but my response was a Definite NO.

I remember bring pestered a couple of times by a person who was sitting on a separate table in different company who were his crew members. He kept asking Cheryl to dance but didn't seem to grasp that she could not understand what he was saying. After a couple of refusals Cheryl said that she would dance with him just to keep him quiet which she did. Soon the night came to an end but not before being invited to Agga's friend's house for a night cap. I always found the Faroes and Danish people extremely welcoming and friendly. We didn't stay too long as we didn't want to impose and we soon returned to the Lady.

It's was nice having my wife onboard as she could see for herself the work that is involved in my chosen career as a trawlerman. Although, I must admit, this type of fishing (purse seining) seems an easier option to the other types of trawling I have been involved with. However, it still came with many dangers.

The two weeks have passed very quickly since picking Cheryl up at Alborg Airport and then sailed from Hirtshals and then onward to the Minch, in search of mackerel. I know it must have been difficult for her travelling by herself and then saying goodbye after taking her back to the airport. I know that she has and always will stand by me in any decision I choose to do to put meals on the table and a roof over our head. I know being a fisherman's wife can't be easy. Having your man at home for a short while, then all alone to make decisions on keeping the family together. Not all marriages lasted because of the loneliness that they endure whilst the men were at sea. I've really enjoyed her company and I think she had enjoyed our time together too.

I am feeling a bit low as Cheryl has now gone home. I felt helpless the first couple of days with Cheryl being seasick then she got used to the noise and all the rolling movements. I'm sure that she enjoyed herself. Saying goodbye to her always leaves a tear in my eye, but now I'm rejoining the ship in Hirtshals. Within half an hour of rejoining the Lady we were out of the Harbour and into the Skagerrak, heading towards the fishing grounds once more.

Unfortunately, within forty-eight hours, we were heading back into Hirtshals. As we shot the net, we think we became tangled up on a wreck which resulted in us losing most of the top net but we managed to save the bottom which contained all the lead weights and metal clip rings. As we did not have a spare purse net on board, several telephone calls went out to enable us to borrow a net. We did manage to borrow a purse net which was much smaller than ours and I seem to remember the net had previously been used for catching pilchards or sardines. This didn't really matter as we still managed to catch three or four hundred tons and a few times we managed to catch a decent haul of herring. We landed the first catch in St. Malo and on the next occasion we landed in Ijmuiden in Holland which is where we had problems with their Custom Officers.

Raymond Evans told me to let the Faroese crew know that they must put there bond back in the ship's locker as he had heard that the rummages would be coming onboard and they usually did a full search of the ship looking for hidden bond such as smokes, baccy etc. A few of the crew took notice of the warning but not everyone agreed to do this. I picked one of my pillow cases and chucked my bond into it but not before putting my name on the back cover. I popped to the bond locker and gave my stuff to Ray but I had kept aside maybe three packets of smoke for my own use. If the rummages are like the ones we had in Grimsby, then we were in for a rough ride, as they say.

Outside of Ijmuiden a pilot cutter came to meet us. A pilot came on board and I escorted him to the bridge then scarpered before I was asked to steer the ship by hand. I needn't have worried as Garry got the job. We soon approached a lock but just as we were about to enter, a small pilot boat, similar to the ones we have in the Humber, approached us. As soon as the craft came alongside approximately fifteen persons, male and female, boarded us.

Whilst we were penned in the lock gates, I was told to go to my cabin where a custom officer would meet me. After a few minutes the Customs Officer (rummager) asked me if this was my cabin and I replied that it was. He then asked me whether I had any bond and I replied that I only had what was in my locker. I was just about to open the drawer, when I was told to just stand in my cabin. He soon discovered I had been telling the truth. He then proceeded to look in my wardrobe, finding nothing. I had a spare under bunk locker which I used with a laundry bag to put my dirty clothes and shitty pants in. He looked at me more or less thinking that I was a scruffy sod. I usually did my laundry, maybe twice a week but I had simply forgotten to put them in the washing machine. He soon left me, thanked me for my time and then went on to his next mission.

All the English had put their bond into the locker. Of course, I mean those who smoked. Lots of the Faroese didn't heed the warning and preferred to hide there's under the whaleback steering flat but these were soon discovered. A few wouldn't admit to hiding there's in such places which only prolong the outcome but in time these people owned up. The result was that the hidden bond was confiscated and the individual were reprimanded.

Eventually, we arrived at our berth next to a papermill and under the cover of darkness we soon discharged the herring. After landing I rolled in for a few hours. Some of the Faroese took a taxi into Amsterdam to buy or look at some gardening magazines, I should imagine.

When I woke up at around 0900 hours I ventured onto the afterdeck where I noticed a large van which had its back doors open. I then I heard a voice ask whether I wanted to buy anything. Curious, I went ashore by the gangway, looked into the back of the wagon and was asked again; 'Did I want anything?' All the items were Phillips which was a big Electrical Company in Holland. I ended up buying a radio, television and cassette player for about twenty quid and I must say I had this for a long time after I left the Lady.

By teatime we were on our way back towards the Isle of Wight where big catches were bring caught by the pursers. We worked many a time with the St Loman which was similar to The Lady with part English and Danish crew members.

Apparently, the mackerel have now moved south with plenty of shoals reported at the Scilly Isles. We had been around the Isle of Man and then onto the Scilly Isles where fishing became slack once more. We have had a couple of nets when we shot containing pilchards', sardines with skad, (horse mackerel). We had a small job on our hydraulics and we called into Plymouth once more.

To this day I still don't know what had happened but Garry left the ship saying, 'That's me done!' He said he had enough. This was when I moved up a grade by became the flag mate.

I am now the 2nd mate, sat on the bridge steaming towards the Butt of Lewis. I have a Faroese watchmate with me on my watch. As it was quiet in the shipping lanes, I started to reflecting how my life had changed as, just over six months ago, I had been in a Ross Cat Boat and the equipment was so different to what I am using now.

On the Cat Boats the ships wheel had eight spokes and you had to stand behind it, looking up into a binnacle compass which looked like a Periscope. Just to the side of the ships wheel we had a mark 21 Decca navigator which allowed us to know our position whilst at sea. It worked on the principle of having radio beacons all along the European coastline which transmitted signals to our apparatus. We also had a Decca plotter and every skipper had their own which contained the information they had gathered over the years., just behind the ships wheel we had two times Kelvin Hughes fish finders which were primitive to what we use today but quite effective. A chart room with a radio room were directly behind the helmsman at the wheel which in turn led into the Skippers cabin. Before I move on, we had a radar on the portside which gave us a coastline readout as well as picking ships out. We had three people at any given time as watchkeepers although this would change if we had any work to complete on the main deck. For all the crew we had one toilet and only a single shower and a sit-down bath which we used mainly for washing our clothes by hand, The equipment on the ship I am now on was modern, up-to-date and luxurious in comparison.

The Skipper had just about given up hope of catching any fish when we caught a decent haul of mackerel. We pumped almost 400 ton on board and with a couple of hundred more on board when HMS JERSEY (Fishery Protection) called our ship up to inform us that they were boarding us to check everything was in order. It didn't interfere with our work as it was mainly to do with paperwork on the bridge. Eventually they left the ship to let us get on with our job.

It was then decided that we would be discharging our catch in Hirtshals, dropping the crew off in Torshavn and eventually sailing to Grimsby to keep our port of registration legal. That time soon came and we proceeded to

Grimsby. We tried to get into the fish docks but there was not enough water to enable us to get in this dock.

We eventually tied up alongside in the Royal Dock. It has been a few months since I sailed from Hull and I've really enjoyed working on this type of vessel which is years' ahead of its time for Grimsby.

We have arranged to meet Agga tonight in the Dolphin Hotel for a few beers. After being home a few hours, it had been time to meet Agga who would be with John Gillibrand who was one of the directors of our ship. We had been in Stella's Bar and within a few hours we had moved on to Sands Club. This was a local nightclub noted for the live entertainment it provided which was run by Tommy Lee and his beautiful wife Joan. We stayed until closing time when Cheryl and I went home and Agga went back to the Grimsby Lady.

A couple of days later I had been summoned down dock to the office which was porta cabin in Tyson's Yard on the North Wall. The accountant, Mr Swales, had asked if a couple of us would paint the fish holds out and we would of course, be paid for doing the job. We agreed and within a couple of days myself, John the cook and a new crew member called Stan, worked from 0900 hours until working from 0900 hours until 1600 hours. We did this for a few days but then it was just myself and the cook, John Langdale. Stan went missing. We were being paid well for painting the tanks. Whilst the ship had been in dock, we had a watch man looking after the ship. When the work on the ship was finished, we were summoned to sail.

Agga and Sverry the Faroese Fishery Skipper and Mate together with the Engineers Marius and Paulus who had been the Chief Engineer were flown in to sail from

Grimsby. The rest of the crew were picked up in Hirtshals. Joining us this trip Agga's son, Marius. He seemed very keen and willing to learn. He had been studying at the Seaman's School in Copenhagen.

Finally, after four weeks in Grimsby we had been ordered to sail. The bonus for me had been that we were in our own port which enabled us to go home every night. A couple of us had been on daily pay as we had been painting the fish tanks. Only John, the cook and myself turned to everyday. Stan did two days and was not seen again until sailing day.

We planned to sail from Grimsby, mid-afternoon, when a man came on board and pinned a piece of paper to the mast which turned out to be a writ. This meant that the ship could not leave the port until it was paid. I believe this was for fuel but a couple of hours later we had two more writs for food stores. Our ships agent Jens Berg had been contacted and after a few hectic telephone calls and the writs were removed and we were allowed to sail. it seems that too many people were taking money out of the pot without paying the bills. Pleased to leave the port once more and we are now heading to Hirtshals.

I took the second watch out of dock and we are heading towards Hirtshals to drop off the purse net and pick up the rest of the crew. No sooner had we tied up when a man came on board pinning a note on the mast which again turned out to be another writ, this time for fuel. Within a few hours it had been taken off the mast and the monies paid which would allow us to sail. Andy Jensen came with us to Hirtshals but didn't sail with us to the fishing grounds.

The Faroese crew duly arrived. Stan, the new crew member, had been sharing the cabin with Finnur. When Finnur went to his cabin, he quickly came out speaking to Agga and Ray who both had been in the messdeck area. He told them that his cabin had been wrecked with all the seating area ripped out, both mattresses were in the same state. Stan could be found flaked out on the cabin floor.

Words were soon exchanged and the Police came on board to remove Stan, who we never saw again. I believe he was hospitalised in Denmark for quite some time. The seats were then sent ashore and within two hours were returned recovered and new mattresses were installed. I thought that we might have another night ashore and I was surprised when we sailed.

It is my second season fishing for mackerel. We were receiving good reports of large mackerel being caught around Rhona which is a small Island just off the North end of Scotland. With a fair wind and clear skies, we were sailing at just under 15 knots. The clear skies meant that we could watch the shooting stars pass through the earth's atmosphere, leaving a trail of light. As quick as you spotted one, they disappeared. Within thirty-six hours we were heading to Aalesund. This will feel strange having not been to Norway since we were chucked out due to quotas. We were heading to the same port with the St Loman.

We are running up the coastline towards Aalesund to discharge our catch. We had a magnificent show of the northern lights with mainly green and a lime colour dancing away in the night. Lights flickered from the shoreline which were mainly from the buoyage systems and a few cars making their way up the Mountain side.

Another memory was the last time we had been near Aalesund we were going towards Tromso to drop a man off who had fallen down the engine room ladders, breaking his leg and wrist which had happened through drink. This often happened as we made our way to the fishing grounds. The bond would be issued and it would be party time. Many a fall or an argument happened at this time. All through drink which often resulted in injuries.

I recall another occasion when I was a deckie and on a different ship, I had come off the Bridge and went below towards my cabin but not before popping my head in the cook's cabin. No sooner had I entered the cabin and a certain person lunged at me with a gutting knife. With my right hand I instantly shielded myself but not before sustaining a deep cut across my palm. Instinctively my reflexes kicked in and I twatted my attacker, maybe twice and he went down like a lump of coal. A towel had been passed to me which I wrapped tightly around the cut. The man accused me of sleeping with his wife which did not happen. He apologised the next day and blamed the drink for his behaviour. I remember the was Mate, George Hornsby, who padded up my hand to stop it bleeding. I didn't realise how difficult it would be to rely on my left hand as I am right-handed. It was especially difficult rolling a cigarette. However, it didn't stop me working as I became third man down the fish room for a week or so until the cut started its healing process. During this time, I had been smoking tailor made cigarettes.

Soon we were approaching the inlet in to Aalesund. A pilot took us alongside and within an hour we had started to discharge. By lunchtime we had sailed again towards Rhona where we had one or two good catches of decent sized Mackerel which made a good price.

I had been away from home for quite a while and I made a big mistake by telephoning home just after tea (via a link call ship to shore radio). No one had mobiles or laptops like we have today. I had been speaking to Cheryl and I heard my daughter and she wanted to know who was on the phone. She passed the phone to my daughter who said that she couldn't remember what I looked like. Cheryl then told me that the children at school had been teasing her and were being cruel, telling her that and we had got divorced and not told her. They told her that she didn't have a father and she was very upset by the whole thing.

I finished my call home and went straight to see Ray and told him about the call. I told him that I must go home. The next day we arrived in Hirtshals and the arrangements were made for me to go home. We landed the catch, the ship sailed about 2000 hours and another crew member and myself had been put into a hotel for the night. The next morning, we were on our first connection making our way home.

I arrived home just before midnight and the house was in complete darkness. I knocked on the door and light came on in the hallway. Cheryl asked; 'Who is it?' I told her it was me and she said; 'Why didn't you let me know you were coming home!' I explained that I wanted to surprise her and I told her that I let Tracy (Cheryl's sister) know but asked her not to say anything.

I put my flight bag in the kitchen and went upstairs to say hi to Matthew. He was fast asleep and just murmured. I kissed his head and then left his room. Slowly I walked in to Eleanor's room and softly whispered to her, saying; 'Who hasn't got a daddy?' Although fast asleep she raised her hand in the air saying; 'ME!' I left the room, chuckling as I went to tell Cheryl what had happed. Within a few minutes we heard her calling her brother telling him she had seen dad in her room and within moments they were both running downstairs saying that she had just heard me speaking to her. They were absolutely beside themselves to see me and were over the moon to see me. Eventually they went back to bed.

I had a bite to eat, a cup of tea, emptied my pockets on the mantlepiece and made my way for a quick bath. Cheryl removed all the monies and took them upstairs. It is a good job that she did as during the early morning, some local low life and his mate burgled our house gaining entry through the downstairs toilet window. It was a few years later that discovered the names of the culprits, who used to pass our house on a regular basis.

Whilst I had been at home the Fisheries Minister cut our quota to 200 ton of mackerel per week which wasn't profitable to earn a decent living for a ship like the Grimsby Lady. I had purchased a Fishing News from the Newsagents and it contained an article on the second page saying '**GRIMSBY LADY RETURNS TO NORWAY**'.

I had been involved in this venture for about twelve months and I had enjoyed every aspect of the job. To say I was shocked and disappointed is an understatement. I made my way to see Mr Swales on the docks to show him the article. He immediately got on the telephone to Mr Fred Parkes telling him what had been printed in the Fishing News. I was in a dream like state when I received a call from the agent in Hirtshals, asking if I wanted my gear sending home. I replied I most definitely did.

Three days later, I received a call from my Bank at Riby Square telling me that several bags had been delivered to them. Could I please collect them as soon as possible. It was my gear from the ship.

Within a week or so I had been back in a Cat Boat earning a living but this time as a trawlerman. (Full story in Chapter Seven). Unfortunately, this job didn't last much longer and one trip in the Ross Lynx I had been relieving the regular bosun. We were fishing near Foula when we hit a bag of Dogfish. These become dead weight and are difficult to pull on board. After a while, we managed to get the net under control using a rope as a snorkeler, using a bowline knot. We eventually, but slowly used two ropes, heaving on one then releasing the other. It was whist the second heave had been lowered that the trainee on the other rope took his turns off the barrel. My hand was trapped in the knot and I tried to pull my hand away. I could feel myself being pulled over the ships rail and I pushed my knees on the ship's bulwarks, using all my might to stop me going over the side. Arty Musson, who was one of the deckies, quick wittingly, put the rope over the winch barrel, stopping the net going any further outboard. I came away from the ships rail and when I removed my glove, I had lost the end of my middle finger, bruising the rest of my hand and both knee caps.

Within three hours I was put ashore in hospital. The next day travelling home. On arriving home shock set in.

I was home for seven months with this injury and I didn't have a regular berth but did a few trips here and there. I remember being in the Ross Zebra with Paddy McCarthy relieving for two trips when after the first trip the other bosun told me that he was coming back early. My response, 'I'm doing the next trip as well!' He didn't like it and he didn't get his way. I did a few trips here and there.

After being back in the Cat Boats a message came over the airwaves that when the ships come back in dock this trip, they would not be sailing again, due to running costs etc. I had been in the Panther with Freddy Hodson and being one of the first ships to land when the Lumpers went on strike. The crews were offered £30 to land their own catch. I helped unloaded maybe ten of the ships receiving the landing money as soon as the ship was discharged. One of the last to land had been my old ship the Ross Jackal. I had made up with my old skipper and we were friends for years until his untimely death. Both his stepsons helped to discharge the ships and it was a nice bit of pocket money for both Paul and John Ferrand.

The next few days were the most worrying of times. Should I go to fish out of Spain, as many were doing? Or do I go into standby boats out of Lowestoft? The answer appeared in our local paper within a few days. The Cat Boats were going to be converted into Oil Rig Standby Boats and were being operated by a company called CAM SHIPPIING.

Random Memory

After the demise of our fishing industry, I had sailed in the Cat boats which had been converted to oil rig standby. It was a job, but I detested it, in more ways than one. The only good thing about the job was that it paid the bills and kept the wolves from the door.

On one voyage having been away for 42 days, we came in dock. Pete Costello who had been the Ship's Husband, called me into his office. He told me that a job had come up which was teaching other countries how to fish both pelagic and demersal, fishing out of Nigeria and the contract was for twelve-month's. He wanted to know whether it was something I would be interested in. I literally jumped at the chance, signing onto the Ross Illustrious which was a deep-water freezer vessel.

We had to do trials, first working by her for three or four days and we eventually sailed to the Westwards. There we caught 20. baskets of mixed fish and a few shore workers who were working on the ship, came to the cod ends, rubbing their hands, thinking they would get a decent fry up to take home how wrong were. The skipper shouted on the tannoid system that the fish was for the crew only. After a couple of days we returned, docking this time in Grimsby after sailing from Hull.

Whilst at home we had to go to see Dr Renfrew regarding a cocktail of injections. I can recall we had injection in both arms and they included Cholera, Yellow Fever and Black Water Fever. I went to the Doctors Clinic with a couplle of the Crew and having had our injections we were told not to drink any alcohol. I duly went home feeling like shit I got my head down hoping that I would feel better soon. However, the other two lads ended up in hospital as they ignored the doctor and after a couple of pints or so became extremely ill.

A couple of days later I had asked for a copy of the contract as I wanted to know how our earnings would be sent home. I made this request for sight of the contract several times without any response. I made a point of asking to see the contract as, after a home visit from Dave Ferrand (my father in-laws' brother) he told me not to go as although the earnings were very good, it was impossible to take any earnings out of the country. The next day I signed off the ship. When the ship arrived in Nigeria, I heard that the person who was organised the venture, had been found dead on the Beach. What a lucky escape that was and I am pleased that I listened to the advice given.

Photographs of Me
at Various Stages
Thoughout My Life

With Cheryl [Wife]

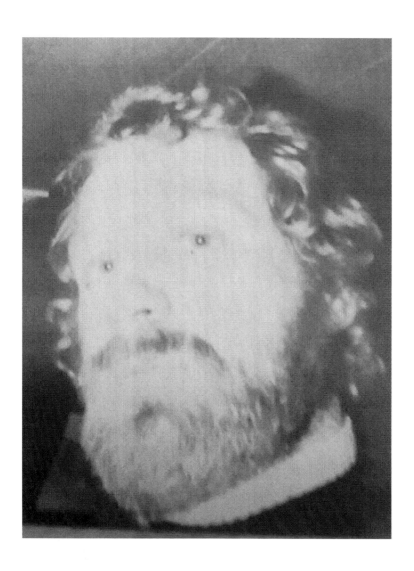

My Good Friend Tommy Fisher and Me!

Tommy Fisher and Magnus Ganson

Ron Telford, Two? Three? Four?
Ducko and Scarborugh John

Garry Evans

Skipper Raymond Evans and Skipper Agga Garvastova

Enjoying a Meal on the Grimsby Lady

The Crew Enjoying a Meal on the Grimsby Lady

Good friend Graham Hobson and Ron Telford
at Grimsby Fisherman's Reunion
September 2023

Mrs Gill Ross (Wife of the late John Carl Ross of the Ross Trawler Dynasty) reviewing the on-going work on the Ross Tiger. She is such a lovely lady who works tirelessly for various charities.

Trawlers Tied Up in Grimsby Dock

Pier Pavilion, Cleethorpes

C.4328

Cleethorpes Pier and Submarine Pub

Recognition and Gratitude

When I first went to sea, I can remember all the old sailors who were patient and taught me their trade. Snowy Richardson, John Royal and Pete Richardson, who sailed on either the Boston Weelsby or the Princess Elizabeth which were the first vessels I sailed on at 15 years 10 months.

There were many other who impressed me in various ways although I cannot bring to mind all of their names. Here are a few I do recall:

Bill Patterson

Bill Smith

Odd job Goddard

Carnation George

SKIPPERS

Bill Ferrand

Tom Whitcombe

David Ferrand

Billy Balls

Lenny Smith

Andy Jensen [Greenland Ghost]

Barry Stokes

Wally Stokes

Barry McCall [Big Bag]

Pete Fenty

Wally Nutten [The Nut]

Albert Hollington [Bonzo]

Paddy McCarthy

Albert Brown

Ray Evans

Roy Kurz [Twisted Lips]

Dave Scott [Kojak]

Dennis Avery

Bob Penketh

Derek Brown

MATES

Colin Quickfall	Garry Evans
Ron Stoneman	Izzy Woods
Sid Carter	Pete Almond
Dave Sherriff	Tom Smith
Jimmy Greene	Jack Jones
Lenny Bruce	Mally Smith
Johnny Harper	Tom Penketh

DECK HANDS
- too numerous to remember them all but include:

Tommy Fisher	Tom Smith
Jerry Proudlove	Johnny Walker
Dave Pratt	Ken Ford
Paul Duxon [Ducko]	Colin Lee
Baz Bridges	Fred Powles
Jack Quantril [Uggy]	Dave Powles

COOKS
- some of the many cooks:

Mick Major	Dixie Loveridge
Harold Bott	Egg and bacon Smithy
Alec Pye	Alec Webb
Tom Jones	George Drury
John Smith	George [Nicho] Nicholson
Tommy Burton	Pete Bowman

Glossary of Trawling Terminology

Aft The extreme end of the vessel from the bow.

Amidships The area near or at the middle of the vessel.

Backhander A sum of money given to a friend who was 'out of a ship' (i.e., not working). The man giving the backhander was known as a 'hovel'.

Backing round When trawling, this is the act of turning the ship 180 degrees round to port.

Backing off When trawling, this is the act of altering course to port.

Backstrop A wire which has three eyes, two attached to the back of the otter board, the third holds the Kelly's eye which is instrumental when attaching/detaching the otter boards.

Banana Link A shaped link that accommodates the large bow shackle which joins the two trawl door brackets, and to which the warp is attached.

Baskets A round container made from wicker in which fish catch was roughly calculated. There were approximately 3 baskets to 2 kits. A kit when measured out on the fish market was equal to 10 stone (63.5 kilo) in weight.

Becket A term used for a number of different items. The main double becket fits around the cod end and allows a large catch to be brought onboard efficiently in manageable quantities.

Bight A loop formed in a rope or wire.

Blocking up The action of containing the two warps in the towing block aft when shooting the gear.

Bobbins The heavy string of steel and rubber spheres which act as the footrope and allows the gear to stay in contact with the seabed.

Bogs The aluminium or composite floats on the headline. In Grimsby they were called 'cans'.

Bolsh A soft three strand rope attached to the leading edges of the trawl wings which is then fastened to the headline or footrope.

Bosun Short for Boatswain who was a watch keeper and in charge of the deck in the absence of the Mate.

Brackets The two triangular steel fixtures on the otter boards to which the towing warps are clipped/unclipped.

Braiding needle A small wooden instrument used to repair/braid net, when loaded with twine.

Bridge The upper part of the superstructure which contains the wheelhouse.

Bridge Telegraph The mechanical communication instrument for conveying engine movement from the wheelhouse to the engine room.

Bunk A seaman's bed.

Busters A round hotcake baked by many Cooks, usually eaten with a cup of tea between mealtimes.

Butterfly One of the components of the Dan Leno arrangement; holds the toe leg wire and the headline wire.

Cables Lengths of wire between the trawl and the trawl doors. In Grimsby they were called 'sweeps'.

Cable drum The main wire holders on the starboard and port sides of the winch for housing the warps.

Chief Engineer The head qualified Engineer in charge of and responsible for the engines and all mechanical, hydraulic and pumping equipment.

Clumpers Old cut down sea boots used as 'slippers.'

Clog Additional weight added to otter board shoe. Helps prevent the wear and tear on shoe.

Cod end The final part of a trawl net which is made of strong double twine. It contains the fish as the opening is tied off by use of the cod line.

Cod line knot A slip type of knot used specifically on the cod end. It closes off the open end but can be easily released when the catch comes onboard.

Coming round When trawling, this is the act of turning the ship 180 degrees round to starboard.

Coming to When trawling, this is the act of altering course to starboard.

Dan Lenos A part of the iron gear that is towed ahead of the main trawl attached to the ground cable. It consists of a 24-inch steel sphere through which a spindle is housed, this is connected to the butterfly section which holds the headline and toe legs.

Deckhand A proficient and usually experienced fisherman whose role is specifically deck work especially during fishing operations.

Deckie learner A young apprentice type deckhand.

Derrick A heavy duty steel arm attached to the foremast used to heave the cod ends outboard by means of a block and wire commonly referred to as a 'yo yo' wire.

Dippy giggle An odd physical condition often experienced by those who work on deck for long hours in extreme conditions. Its effect makes men laugh when generally there is little to laugh at.

Donkey The salt water hose provided to the fish washer from the engine room sea water pump. Old term for a pump engine of less than one horse power.

Door chain The heavy duty chain secured to the gallows which is used when disengaging the trawl doors during the hauling and shooting operation.

Double sheave The heavy lift block with two rollers secured on the foremast and used with the tackle hook to bring the bag of fish inboard.

Duck Pond The lowest area on the deck where the working deck meets the raised after area and where the largest scupper is situated to allow water shipped onboard to flow out.

Fasteners Wrecks or other seabed obstructions that the trawler's gear can be caught up on and damaged or lost.

Fathom A measurement of water depth equal to 6 feet (1.83 metres).

Fireman Assistant to the Chief or Second Engineer.

Fish room The below deck section of the vessel specifically designed to hold/preserve the catch.

Fish room man A deckhand who managed the fish room.

Fleet A process whereby lengths of net are brought sequentially onboard by use of lifting gear.

Floats Aluminium or plastic spheres used to float open the headline of the trawl whilst being towed on the seabed.

Footrope The heavy-duty string of steel/rubber bobbins used to weigh the bottom of the trawl onto the seabed.

Force 4-5 Wind speed as stated on the Beaufort Scale where winds of between 13 and 24mph are experienced.

Fore Towards the bow.

Foredeck The part of the working deck between the duckpond and the whaleback.

Foul gear To have a problem with the trawl/ tangled gear.

Frap Having a problem; in a bit of chaos.

Galley The vessel's kitchen where all food is prepared and cooked.

Galley boy The Cook's assistant, the most junior rating onboard.

Gallows The horseshoe shaped large steel structures sited close to the ships rail, both aft and forward, through which the warps ran during hauling, shooting and towing of the gear.

Gash Extra sleep when watch below, due to no work until hauling time.

G Link A heavy duty G shaped link which is used to connect/disconnect the trawl warps to the otter boards.

Gilguy A wire used through a block on the wheelhouse to fleet the volume of net inboard which include the square, belly/baitings and lengtheners.

Gilson hook The hook used on the end of the Gilson wire used for most heaving tasks other than the final lift inboard of a bag of fish.

Ground cable The sweep wires located between the otter boards and the Dan Lenos.

Guiding on gear The mechanism fitted at the front of the winch which spools the warps evenly on the cable drums.

Gutting The action of removing the innards of the fish in order to prevent them spoiling.

Haddock Rash An irritable skin condition which causes a rash to the hands, wrists, forearms, when gutting haddocks which have sand, grit in the gut.

Hammerlock A modern type of shackle that comes in two parts with a locking pin.

Hauling The retrieving of the fishing gear after being towed for a given period of time.

Headline The wire reinforced top of the mouth of the trawl net which houses the spherical floats.

Helm A common term given to the process of altering the ship's rudder to change the direction of the ship's heading.

Hopper A machine used to transfer the raw livers from the deck to the liver house aft, operated by steam.

Jummy Lump A hurtful physical condition to a deckhand's wrists caused by excessive work, in the main gutting.

Keep A steel link sliced into the ground cable which, when stopped in the Kelly's eye allows the otter boards to be attached/detached.

Kelly's eye An item of ironware used within the components of a full set of gear, used specifically to capture the cable keep thereby allowing the otter boards to be connected/disconnected.

Knocking out The act of releasing the warps from the towing block.

Leeside The side opposite to the weather which gave some shelter to those working on deck.

Leggo aft A colloquial command meaning to let the warps go free from the towing block to enable hauling of the gear to take place.

Length A measurement of 25 fathoms on the trawl warps marked by intertwining rope into the wire.

Lengtheners A section of double net between the belly/baitings and the cod end. It allows space within the trawl if a large catch is made.

Liver baskets The baskets used to save the livers in during the gutting of the fish.

Liver house A section aft within which large steam operated boilers rendered the raw livers into liver oil. In some vessels the plant was situated forward.

Mate The ship's deck officer junior only to the Skipper.

Messroom The area dedicated to where the crew ate their meals and enjoyed recreation.

Officer's Mess The area onboard specifically for use by the Officers for eating/recreation.

Oilskins Waterproof clothing worn by the deckhands. Rubber, plastic suits or all-in-one frock – like garments.

Otter boards The 11 x 5 foot steel and wood constructed doors used to provide the horizontal opening to the trawl when being towed on the seabed. They were apparently named after one of the first steam trawlers to use them.

Pan of shackles A common name to describe a meat/vegetable stew.

Paying out When the warps are running outboard during the shooting of the gear.

Portside The side of a vessel that lies on your left-hand side when facing the bow (forward).

Pot of spesh Short for 'special' – a pot of tea made with the crew members' own tea rather than the Company issue.

Pound An area of the deck closed off using boards to restrict fish movement.

Preventor chain/ Restraining chain A heavy duty chain with one end secured to the gallows with the other end being free to secure the otter board during hauling/shooting of the gear.

Rigging A fixture consisting of three heavy duty wrapped wires attached to the deck at the bottom and diverging at one point on the mast below the crosstree to form a 'ladder' to climb up/down.

Scratching on Signing on the ship's Articles (a Contract) before sailing.

Scuppers Openings in the ship side plating at deck level, to allow any sea water taken onboard to run away freely. They were also a means of getting rid of guts, debris etc.

Second Engineer A qualified watchkeeping engineer junior to the Chief Engineer.

Selvedge's The edges of a net section, laced together to seal and reinforce sections of the trawl.

Sheave A roller type block through which the warps or wire can freely run through, as the ones attached at the fore and aft gallows.

Shooting The operational process of sending the fishing gear to the seabed.

Sitting Term used at mealtimes for the times the crew would eat i.e., 1200 to 1230 first sitting/1230 to 1300 second sitting.

Sittings or Settings Short lengths of twine used to secure the bolsh on the trawl wings to the headline or footrope.

Skipper The Senior Officer onboard with sole responsibility for the safety and profitability of the vessel.

Snacker A Deckie Learner.

Snottler A heavy rope used for hauling in the bellies of the net when something very heavy had been trawled up.

Splice A process whereby a rope/wire is repaired or when an eye needs to be formed.

Splodge Often used as a nickname for the younger members of the crew – Deckie Learner or Galley Boy.

Starboard The side of a vessel that lies on your right-hand side when facing the bow (forward).

Tannoid A loud hailer communication system, which links the bridge to a number of areas on the ship.

Third Hand A uncertified proficient experienced deckhand who assumes a watch keeping role usually overseen by the Skipper.

Toe leg wire A wire which forms part of the ground gear connecting the footrope to the Dan Leno.

Tow The action of trawling the fishing gear along the seabed.

Towing block Is the fix point at the stern into which the warps are safely retained while the fishing gear is being towed on the seabed. It allows the vessels to be manoeuvred by keeping the warps clear from the propeller/rudder.

Trawl The complete net part of a trawler's fishing gear.

Treacle duff A common dish, a pudding which can be produced as a savoury or with treacle as a sweet.

Twine The 'string like' material used in the production of netting.

Two blocks The term used when anything being lifted by a derrick cannot go any higher.

Wake The disturbed path of water created by the ship's propeller.

Warps Heavy duty wire that the fishing gear was towed on.

Watch A period of duty.

Whipping drums The outer barrels on a winch on which most wire/rope heaving operations take place.

Winch The main mechanical power source on deck to heavy/lift weights. It is fundamental to the hauling and shooting of the fishing gear.

Wing rubbers Rubber discs slotted onto wires which are attached to the main bobbins and form the footrope.

Wireless Operator The communications officer responsible for all transmissions on behalf of the Skipper and has total responsibility for the maintenance and repair of all electronic equipment i.e., radio, radar, echo sounders.

Also by Ron Telford

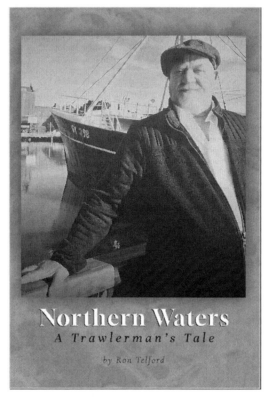

Paperback ISBN 9781800945555 and Kindle eBook

Bosun, Ron Telford is keen to preserve the social history of an industry that no longer exists; believing that some record should be kept showing the dangers and risks that the men of Grimsby, Hull and other ports of the UK endured to put 'fish on the table'.

In this book of true tales, Ron starts at the beginning of his career as a young deckie learner, progressing to deck hand and attendance at Nautical College to obtain a Third Hand's Certificate.

Ron relives the trip and describes events from setting sail and as the trip commences to the sudden changes in weather and the obstacles that had to be overcome. He remembers well the skill of the Skipper, who had to find and catch the fish, the teamwork of the crew who had to clean and store the catch and the expertise of the engineers who kept the ship mechanically sound.

Ron Telford also recalls the many problems encountered with the weather, equipment, trawl, net mending, various types of fish, the meals and the camaraderie amongst the crew. And of course, he recollects homelife - once the trip was over, having only 72 hours ashore - together with the heartache of having to leave loved ones in order to earn a living.

---

*Available worldwide from Amazon
and all good bookstores*

Michael Terence
Publishing

www.mtp.agency

www.facebook.com/mtp.agency

@mtp_agency

Printed in Great Britain
by Amazon

36041328R00135